Frankenstein the Panto

It's a hard life for little orphan Heidi in Pumpernickel's Tavern. The greedy innkeeper and his bossy wife treat her like a slave. And that's not all ... up in his castle, gormless Count Dracula and his gummy grandmother are planning a dinner party, with Heidi as the main course!

Luckily, she's got the audience and other friends to help: her faithful dog Kodak, her best friend Frankie Stein and the handsome Prince Ludwig. The Forces of Evil never stand a chance ... especially when Professor Crackpot transforms Frankie into a Superhero!

The only real *horrors* are a party of rowdy schoolgirls under the supervision of Miss Nelly, famed pedagogue and pantomime dame. They're studying how to create havoc ... and they're all fast-learners!

Other titles by David Swan

Aladdin
Ali Baba and the Forty Thieves
Pinocchio
The Sleeping Beauty

FRANKENSTEIN THE PANTO

BY

DAVID SWAN

Noda Pantomimes
(a division of the National Operatic & Dramatic Association)
NODA House, 1 Crestfield Street, London, WC1H 8AU

This script is published by NODA PANTOMIMES, NODA House, 1 Crestfield Street, London WC1 8AU, telephone (01) 837 5655, to whom all enquiries regarding purchase of further copies, licences to perform and record, and current royalty rates should be addressed. NODA PANTOMIMES will also send full details of the many other scripts in this series.

ISBN 0 901318 12 4

NODA PANTOMIMES is a division of NODA LIMITED which is the trading arm of the NATIONAL OPERATIC & DRAMATIC ASSOCIATION, a registered charity devoted to the encouragement of amateur theatre.

First published 1987
Revised and reprinted 1989

Made and printed in Great Britain by
M.D. Print and Design
Unit 9, Castle Brae Business Centre
Peffer Place, Edinburgh

For Pamela and Dennis Quinn

and

In memory of Paul Stephenson,

who would have laughed

Suggestions for Musical Numbers

Most of the suggestions listed here will be familiar to audiences and are therefore more likely to be enjoyed. Authorization to use any copyright songs and music must be obtained from: **The Performing Rights Society Ltd., 29-33 Berners Street, London W1P 4AA.**

Song A	"Hello, Hello There!" *(Bells Are Ringing - Jule Styne)*
Song B	"Master Of The House" *(Les Misérables - Boublil & Schonberg)*
Song C	"Give A Little Whistle" *(Pinocchio - Walt Disney)*
Song D	"Once A Year Day" *(The Pyjama Game - Adler & Ross)*
Song E	The School Anthem *(The Liberty Bell - Sousa)*
Song F	"The Sun'll Come Out Tomorrow" *(Annie - Strouse & Charnin)*
Dance A	Junior Ballet *("Alfred Hitchcock Presents" theme - available on "Television's Greatest Hits, Vol.1", TVT 1100, HMV - Tower London)*
Song G	"Look What Happened To Mabel" *(Mac and Mabel - Jerry Herman)*
Song H	"Ghostbusters" *(Ray Parker Jnr.)*
Song I	The School Anthem *(Reprise)*
Song J	"It's A Hard Knock Life" *(Annie - Strouse & Charnin)*
Song K	"Suddenly, Seymour" *(Little Shop of Horrors - Ashman & Menken)*
Song L	"The Loco-Motion" *(G. Goffin & C.King)*
Song M	Songsheet
Song N	"Once A Year Day" *(Reprise)*
Song O	"I Don't Need Anything But You" *(Annie - Strouse & Charnin)*

CHARACTERS

(in order of appearance)

Herr Pumpernickel	*an innkeeper*	(M)
Frau Pumpernickel	*his wife*	(F)
Frankie	*their servant*	(M)
Heidi	*an orphan (principal girl)*	(F)
Kodak	*her dog*	(M/F)
Buckles	*the prince's valet*	(M/F)
Prince Ludwig	*of Bavaria (principal boy)*	(F)
Professor Crackpot	*a crazy inventor*	(M)
Miss Nelly	*a headmistress (dame)*	(M)
Bridget Bloggs	*a schoolgirl*	(F)
Mabel Crumb	*a schoolgirl*	(F)
Agnes Swipe	*a schoolgirl*	(F)
Constance Swot	*a schoolgirl*	(F)
Ethel Ready	*a schoolgirl*	(F)
Count Dracula	*a vampire*	(M)
Granula	*his grandmother*	(F)

Chorus and Dancers: Citizens of Bavaria, schoolgirls, bats and ghosts.
16 Principals: 5 male, 9 female and 2 male/female.
Some doubling up possible: Herr & Frau Pumpernickel with Dracula and Granula.

ACT I

Scene 1	Pumpernickel's Taverna, Bavaria	*(full set)*
Scene 2	Outside Pumpernickel's Taverna	*(front of tabs)*
Scene 3	The Haunted Bedroom	*(half set)*
Scene 4	A Hallway in Pumpernickel's Taverna	*(front of tabs)*
Scene 5	Professor Crackpot's Laboratory	*(full set)*

ACT II

Scene 1	Dracula's Castle	*(full set)*
Scene 2	Song Sheet	*(front of tabs)*
Finale		

Note: The scenes are designed to blend into one another: full set, front of tabs, full set, etc. They offer the opportunity for elaborate and imaginative staging but are equally suitable for a small-scale production.

Description of Characters

Herr Pumpernickel is extremely oily and obsequious. He panders to anyone with money and willingly squeezes pennies from the poor. Though harsh on Heidi, he is not a 'heavy' villain and should be played humourously.

Frau Pumpernickel his prodigal wife, is very generous ... with herself. She has an unquenchable thirst for vulgar finery and thinks that her coarse manners are the height of etiquette. They are a well-matched, selfish, couple.

Frankie should be a believably real person. He is kind-hearted, humourous and naturally likeable ... the audience must regard him as their friend. He takes neither his role as the cheeky servant nor the dumb monster seriously.

Heidi is exploited by the Pumpernickels because she is a helpless orphan. Despite this, she is not a pathetic character ... she is humorous, hard working, forthright and uncomplaining.

Kodak is a challenging, non-speaking part. The performer should incorporate as many 'doggy' mannerisms as possible into his performance: sniffing, licking, scratching, etc.

Buckles is practical, down to earth and doesn't suffer fools gladly. He is older and wiser than Ludwig and often has to bail him out of awkward situations.

Prince Ludwig attempts to be very grand but is too inexperienced to be convincingly regal. He is shy, tends to be forgetful and obviously relies heavily on Buckles.

Professor Crackpot a 'nutty', absent-minded professor. He should speak with a phoney, but intelligible, German accent. His dishevelled clothes and unkept hair are proof that great minds have little time for personal appearance!

Miss Nelly is brazen, effervescent and quick-witted. She is totally unshockable as far as her girls are concerned ... we should get the impression that their behaviour is the result of her careful training.

Bridget Bloggs is a dumb-blonde and "gold-digger", well trained in the art of trapping her man. She should look 'sexy' in her uniform and believe that she is the focus of all male attention.

Mabel Crumb is a lazy loafer. She couldn't care less and this should be reflected in her slovenly appearance and sloppy mannerisms.

Agnes Swipe is a hyperactive "super-brat". She is a fast-moving, quick-tempered bully with a well developed criminal mind.

Constance Swot is teacher's pet. She appears to be meek and well-behaved but is, in fact, the 'brains' of the gang.

Ethel Ready is a hypochondriac and a moaner. She would love to be the centre of attention but never is. The others constantly push her around.

Count Dracula is basically an upper-class twit. He has impeccable manners and should speak with a very posh, "Sloane Ranger" accent. A failure as a vampire, he would have expired eons ago had it not been for his granny.

Granula looks decrepit but appearances are deceptive: she can leap quickly into action when required. She is more vicious than Dracula and has brains enough for two.

NOTE: None of the schoolgirls have to be played by juveniles.

Act One
Scene 1
Pumpernickel's Taverna - Bavaria

(Full-stage ... see Appendix A. There are stairs U.L. to the first floor of the tavern and beneath this a swing-door with a sign saying "Kitchen". The main door is U.C. and above this is a changeable sign which, at the moment, reads "Pumpernickel's Taverna". There is a window with sky beyond U.R. and another door with a sign saying "LAB". There is a Bar R. which also functions as a Reception Desk later in the scene. On the Bar is a sign saying "Happy Hour" and a bell. Tables and chairs are scattered around the rest of the stage.
The decor of the opening set is "German" and should be bright and cheerful. A mirror hangs on the wall near the Kitchen Door. There are signs everywhere: "Credit? No! Nein! Non! Nee!", "No Nose Blowing On Tablecloths - The Management", "Rooms to Let" "Cash Only", "Menu - Today's Special - Snail Quiche - Sweet and Sour Kraut - Best Wurst"
The Chorus and Dancers are dressed in German peasant costumes. Throughout the opening production number: HERR PUMPERNICKEL pulls steins of beer behind the bar; HEIDI takes trays of beer to the customers; FRAU PUMPERNICKEL and FRANKIE come in and out of kitchen, serving food; KODAK, the dog, scrounges titbits.

SONG A
Principals and Chorus

ALL sing one verse and chorus of the song. The music continues with a short dance - a hands and thigh-slapping 'folk-dance' routine. ALL sing a final, rousing chorus and the song ends. Exit DANCERS. FRANKIE and HEIDI move D.C. and bow. The CHORUS continues eating and drinking unobtrusively. KODAK lies down beneath a table. HERR and FRAU PUMPERNICKEL pick up broom, a mop and a bucket (containing streamers). They move to FRANKIE and HEIDI)

Herr Pump *(handing bucket and mop to FRANKIE)* Alright, you two, that's enough of that ... get back to work.
Frau Pump *(handing broom to HEIDI)* Yes ... I want this place sparkling from top to bottom.
Herr Pump Scrub that floor ...
Frau Pump ... and dust those chairs ...
Herr Pump ... polish that door ...
Frau Pump ... and sweep those stairs ...
Herr Pump ... tote that barge ...
Frau Pump ... and lift that bale ...
Both *(singing)* "Get a little drunk and you land in jail ... *("Ole Man River" - Showboat)*
(They laugh. HERR PUMPERNICKEL returns to the bar, replaces the "Happy Hour" sign with one saying "Reception", and counts money with the aid of a giant calculator. FRAU PUMPERNICKEL exits to kitchen)
Frankie *(curtseying)* Yes sir and madam!
Heidi Oh Frankie, I'm so tired.
Frankie Cheer up, Heidi, we'll soon be finished - you sweep the stairs and I'll mop the floor.

Herr Pump *(shouting)* And be quick about it!

Frankie & Heidi Yes, Herr Pumpernickel! *(HEIDI scurries upstairs)*

Frankie *(D.L.)* Rotten old codger! *(starts to mop the floor and notices the audience)* Oh, hello there - I didn't see you! Have you come to see the show?

Audience Yes!

Frankie That's nice. *(to someone in front row)* Here ... don't chuck your rubbish on the floor. You're not in *local town* now you know! *(to whole audience)* No. This is Bavaria. We like everything kept spotlessly clean here. Even our pigeons have to fly upside down! *(swings mop over shoulder)* Welcome to Pumpernickel's Taverna! *(pointing at HERR PUMPERNICKEL)* That's the landlord of this establishment ... Herr Pumpernickel's the name. *(secretively)* Do you want to know something? *(D.C.)* Well, don't say I told you but *(loud whisper)* he's the meanest, tight-fisted old skinflint in the whole of Bavaria! He'd do anything to make more money. He'd even sell his own grandmother ... oh, no ... he already sold her! He's so stingy he won't even buy a pair of shoes - he just paints his feet black and laces up his toes! *(FRAU PUMPERNICKEL enters from the kitchen with tray and goes to tables)* That's Frau Pumpernickel, his wife. They make a good pair, those two ... he makes the money and she spends it. The only thing she ever put aside for a rainy day was a pair of wellies and a Beecham's Powder!! *(FRAU PUMPERNICKEL exits to kitchen and HERR PUMPERNICKEL moves behind FRANKIE, carrying the calculator and stuffing money into his pocket)* Her favourite book's a cheque book: once she starts one, she can't put it down till it's finished! *(He swings the mop and clouts HERR PUMPERNICKEL in the face ... a drum-beat)* Ooo-er!

Herr Pump What do you think you're doing?

Frankie Just mopping your brow. *(to audience)* He's got ears in the back of his head, that one!

Herr Pump Who are you talking to?

Frankie I was just telling the boys and girls how *kind-hearted* you are.

Herr Pump Boys and girls? *(peering at audience)* Oh yes! There's lots of them - goody, goody gumboils! *(gleefully counting the audience)* Let's see now, that's 300 people *(using calculator)* at £2 a ticket - that's £600! Ha ha! I'm stinking rich!

Frankie No ... you're just *stinking*!

Herr Pump How dare you!

Frankie What I mean is ... there might be 300 people out there, but they haven't all *paid* for their tickets.

Herr Pump Haven't paid???

Frankie There's a big party of *orphans* here tonight.

Herr Pump Orphans??

Frankie *(Soulful music. He tearfully wipes his face with the cloth)* And it's Christmas time. And they haven't got any mummies and daddies to buy them tickets. Ahhh! *(Music stops)*

Herr Pump They haven't got any mummies and daddies? So what??

Frankie *(chirpily)* So we let them in *free*!

Herr Pump *(turning his back on FRANKIE and raging)* Free! Free! I'm going to come down there and chuck you all out!

(Enter FRAU PUMPERNICKEL from kitchen with a large hat. She looks in the mirror and puts it on)

Frankie *(encouraging audience)* Booo!

Audience Booo!

Herr Pump And as for the rest of you ... all those who've paid for their tickets can stay and enjoy the show. And if you don't ... too bad, 'coz I'm not going to give your money back!

Audience Boo!

Herr Pump *(muttering)* Orphans! It's disgusting ... nothing but a lot of good-for-nothing leeches ...

(FRANKIE mimes throwing the bucket of water over HERR PUMPERNICKEL)

Frankie *(to audience)* Shall I give it to him?

Audience Yes.

Frankie Right, here goes. *(FRAU PUMPERNICKEL comes D.S. behind FRANKIE)*

Herr Pump *(continuing over)* blood-suckers ... parasites ... you must think I'm made of money ...

Frankie *(raising bucket)* One! Two! Th...

Frau Pump What do you think you're doing?

Frankie *(lowering bucket, startled)* Nothing, Frau Bumperknickers.

Frau Pump *(hitting him)* "Pumpernickel"! Get back to work! *(FRANKIE kneels D.L. and washes the floor)* Hello, my sweetykins! *(kisses HERR PUMPERNICKEL)*

Herr Pump Hello my sugar-lamb!

Frau Pump Why was everyone booing you, my darling?

Herr Pump It's "Be Kind To Orphans" week ... and they think I'm being unkind!

Frau Pump *(to audience)* Oh but that's *not* true ... we *are* kind to orphans.

Frankie *(encouraging audience)* Oh no you're not!

Herr Pump & Frau Pump Oh yes we are! *(repeat twice)*

Frau Pump Quiet! Stop it! We *are* kind, and I can prove it! *(calling upstairs, harshly)* Heidi!

Heidi *(at top of stairs, with broom)* Yes, Frau Pumpernickel!

Frau Pump Come down here at once! *(HEIDI comes downstairs)* At the double. *(HEIDI hurries)* Hup-one-two-three! Hup-one-two-three!

Frankie *(to audience)* Let's say "hello" to Heidi, everybody. *(waving to Heidi)* Heidi, hi!

All Ho-di-ho!

Frau Pump About time too. What took you so long?

Heidi I'm sorry, Frau Pumpernickel ... I sprained my ankle.

Herr Pump That's a lame excuse! *(laughs)*

Frau Pump Now, Heidi, I want you to tell all the boys and girls about your mummy and daddy!

Heidi *(sadly)* But I haven't got a mummy and daddy!

Frankie Ahhh!

Frau Pump *(to audience)* What did I tell you? *(indicating HEIDI)* An orphan! *(to HEIDI)* Now tell them how kind we are to you.

Heidi *(doubtfully)* You're very kind to me!

Frau Pump Do it properly!

Heidi *(curtseying)* You're very kind to me, sir and madam!

Frau Pump That's better. *(to audience)* Now I hope you're satisfied! *(to HEIDI)* Alright Heidi, you may go and clear the tables.

Heidi *(curtseying)* Thank you, Frau Bumperknickers. *(she collects plates from the tables)*

Frau Pump Watch it! *(to HERR PUMPERNICKEL)* How much money have we made today, my treasure?

Herr Pump *(pulling out banknotes and handkerchief)* Eight hundred and fifty six pounds thirty three pence ... and a snotty handkerchief.

Frau Pump And a snotty handkerchief?

Herr Pump Yes, someone dropped it. I thought we could give it to Heidi for her Christmas Present.

Frau Pump Oh, you're so thoughtful. You're the kindest, cleverest, bestest landlord in the whole of Bavaria.

Herr Pump I try. I try.

SONG B

Principals & Chorus

(During the song, FRANKIE moves up to the main door and changes the tavern sign to read "Nickelpumper's". The song ends. Exit CHORUS. Exit HEIDI to kitchen followed by KODAK. FRANKIE mops the floor once more)

Frau Pump Oh, I'm so excited ... Prince Ludwig is coming to town today! I must go and buy a new hat! *(she snatches the bank-notes from him)*

Herr Pump *(trying to retrieve them)* Hat's are too expensive ... I can't afford it.

Frau Pump Of course you can afford it ... you're my husband.

Herr Pump Yes, and I've been paying for it ever since!

Frau Pump Bye for now. *(exits through Main Door)*

Herr Pump *(chasing after her)* Give me back my money! It's not fair! Come back ... *(exit)*

Frankie *(standing and picking up bucket)* Serves him right, the old skinflint! Well, that's the floor finished! *(moving towards the Reception Desk)* I'd better go and clean the cellars now ... here, wait a minute ... I haven't introduced myself yet, have I? *(sets down bucket)* My name is "Frankie". Hello boys and girls!

Audience *(feebly)* Hello Frankie!

Frankie You don't seem very sure of my name. I said "My name's 'Frankie'". Hello boys and girls!

Audience HELLO FRANKIE!

Frankie That's great! Mind you, I only let my friends call me 'Frankie'. Everyone else has to use my full-name: Frank N. Stein! *(short pause)* No, no, no ... not *that* Frankenstein! I dont look like a big, ugly, green monster with bolts through my neck, do I? Who said "yes"! No, my name's Frank N. Stein - the "N" stands for my middle name. I come from a world-famous family. There's my father, Roger ... he can play "The Sound of Music" on his teeth with a hammer ... you must have heard of him: "Roger and hammer Stein". Oh, they get worse! Then there's my brother - he is the *one* brain in the family ... Ein Stein. And my stupid sister, Phyllis Stein. And last but by no means least, you all know my great, great, great grandfather ... he lived to one hundred and twenty six and was over seven feet tall ... Old Lang Stein! Well, I'd better get on with my work. *(looking into bucket)* Oh, this water's filthy ... I'd better chuck it out. *(Lifts bucket and prepares to throw at audience)* Are you ready to duck? One! Two! Two and a half! *(lowers bucket)* Oh no, I'd better not ... there's a little girl hiding under the seat down here! *(lifting bucket)* It's alright I was just pretending. I'm not going to soak you. *(moving suddenly to another section of audience)* I'm going to soak this lot instead! *(He throws the contents of the bucket at the audience ... the streamers flood out)* Ha ha! That fooled you! See you later. *(exits)*

(BUCKLES enters through Main Door)

Buckles Make way, make way for his Royal Highness: Prince Ludwig of Bavaria.

(Enter PRINCE LUDWIG through the Main Door to C. and immediately reads a speech from the scroll he is carrying)

Ludwig Loyal Subjects, Citizens of Bavaria, lend me your ears ... *(BUCKLES coughs, politely trying to interrupt)* ... I come to bear bad tidings not give good ones ... *(BUCKLES coughs louder)* ... the evil in the night is after us ...

Buckles M'lord?

Ludwig ... and the good ... what is it?

Buckles There isn't anyone here, M'lord!

Ludwig There isn't? *(raises a monocle to his eye and looks around)* Drat! *(strides nervously up and down, followed by BUCKLES)* Where is everybody? This is a matter of life and death! *(stops suddenly and BUCKLES bumps into him)* Ouch! Well don't just stand there, find someone!

Buckles Yes, sir. *(he crosses to the Reception Desk)* Your Highness, there's a bell over here.

Ludwig Well why don't you ring it?

(BUCKLES rings the bell. Enter HEIDI from the kitchen, drying her hands on a towel)

Heidi Hello. Can I help you, sir?

Buckles We must see the master of the house immediately ... it's a matter of life and death!

Heidi Oh dear. There's no-one here but me. Everyone's gone to welcome Prince Ludwig.

Buckles But Prince Ludwig is *here*!

Heidi *(looking around)* Where?

Ludwig I am Prince Ludwig.

Heidi Oh, I'm terribly sorry your majesty ... I didn't recognise you. *(curtseys and stays down)*

Ludwig It's alright, you don't have to curtsey. Let me help you up.

(He gives her his hand and she rises. Romantic music. They gaze at each other and are instantly smitten)

Heidi Thank you, sir.

Ludwig Call me "Ludwig".
Heidi Oh I couldn't do that, sir.
Ludwig Why not?
Heidi You're a prince and I'm only a servant girl.
Ludwig *(using monocle, dreamily)* What's your name?
Heidi Heidi, sir.
Ludwig *(breaking away)* Well, Heidisir, a pretty girl like you shouldn't be left unguarded.
Heidi Why not?
Ludwig *(significantly)* You are in grave danger!
Heidi *(alarmed)* What sort of danger?
Buckles Vampires!
Heidi Vampires???
Ludwig You must be protected.
Heidi Oh, don't worry about me ... I've got a great, big dog to protect me.
Ludwig A dog?
Heidi He's my best friend. You'll like him. I'll call him for you. *(She whistles. Nothing happens)* Oh dear ... I'm sorry about this ... he's a bit deaf, you see. Would you help me whistle for him?
Ludwig Certainly. *(All three whistle. Nothing happens)*
Heidi No. He still can't hear us.
Ludwig *(indicating audience)* Perhaps all the boys and girls will help us?
Heidi What a good idea. *(to audience)* Can any of you whistle? You can? Oh good. I'll count to three and we'll all whistle together. One. Two. Three. *(ALL whistle. Nothing happens)*
Buckles *(to audience)* That's not loud enough!
Ludwig *(to audience)* You'll have to do better than that!
Heidi *(to audience)* Let's try again. Take a really deep breath this time and whistle as loud as you can.

(ALL take a deep breath and whistle. KODAK bounds in from the kitchen and down to the others, wagging his tail)

Heidi *(to audience)* Thank you, everybody. *(to KODAK)* Say "thank you" to the boys and girls. *(KODAK barks at the audience)*
Ludwig What's his name?
Heidi I call him Kodak ... that's because he's always snapping at people!
Ludwig *(stepping back)* Oh!
Heidi Don't worry. He wouldn't hurt a friend. *(raising voice and speaking deliberately)* Kodak, say hello to Prince Ludwig. *(KODAK barks)* You see ... he likes you.
Ludwig Good. *(to KODAK, offering hand)* Paw. *(no reaction)*
Heidi You'll have to speak up a bit.
Ludwig Oh, yes. *(shouting)* PAW! *(KODAK offers paw and he shakes it)* How do you do.
Buckles He won't be much good as a guard dog!
Heidi Why not?
Buckles He can't hear you whistling for him.

Ludwig That's true!
Heidi Oh dear, what are we going to do?
Buckles I know. *(indicating audience)* Why not ask your friends to help?
Heidi That's a good idea. *(to audience)* If you ever hear me shouting for help, will you all whistle for Kodak as loud as you can? Will you?
Audience Yes.
Ludwig Let's have a little practice. *(to BUCKLES)* You pretend to grab her ... *(to audience)* and when you hear Heidi shout for help, whistle for Kodak. O.K.? Off we go! *(BUCKLES pulls an ugly face and grabs HEIDI)*
Heidi Help! Help!
(The audience whistles. KODAK growls, chases BUCKLES around the stage and bites his bottom)
Heidi Here boy! *(KODAK comes to her side. BUCKLES rubs his bottom)*
Ludwig *(to audience)* Well done! Now don't forget ... if you ever hear Heidi calling for help, you have to whistle as loud as you can.

SONG C
Heidi, Ludwig & Buckles

(The song ends. Enter HERR PUMPERNICKEL through the Main Door, closely followed by FRAU PUMPERNICKEL in a garish new hat. They come D.S., bickering)
Herr Pump You're not going to spend another penny, and that's final!
Frau Pump But darling, I need a new dress to match my hat.
Herr Pump You've got a face to match the hat, isn't that enough.
(FRAU PUMPERNICKEL screams and points at LUDWIG)
Herr Pump What is it?
Frau Pump *(ecstatically)* Prince Ludwig! He's my idol!
Ludwig *(bowing deeply)* At your service, maam.
(FRAU PUMPERNICKEL immediately starts rummaging in her bag and pulls out a photograph)
Herr Pump A prince in my humble establishment! *(grovelling on his knees)* Oh your majesty, your highness, your worshipness, your holiness ... how can I ever repay you for your gracious patronage!
(He seizes PRINCE LUDWIG's hand and kisses it fervently. FRAU PUMPERNICKEL seizes his other hand and thrusts a photograph into it)
Frau Pump Look at this, your worship.
Ludwig What's this?
Frau Pump It's your portrait. I carry it with me everywhere. *(handing him a pen)* Please autograph it for me!
(LUDWIG disengages his hand from HERR PUMPERNICKEL, who is still slobbering over it)
Ludwig I shall need something to rest on.
Herr Pump *(offering his back)* Please rest on me, your magnificence, I shall always be most humbly grateful!
(LUDWIG rests on HERR PUMPERNICKEL's back and signs)

Frau Pump *(peeping over his shoulder)* Put "love from".

Ludwig Oh, very well. *(handing photo back)* There we are!

Frau Pump *(reading)* "Love from Prince Ludwig" ... oooo! *(she dashes to Main Door, shouting)* Greta! Marlene! Helga! He's here! Come quick!

(Enter CHORUS through Main Door. FRAU PUMPERNICKEL shows off her autographed portrait to them)

Buckles Your highness, I think it's time to tell everyone the *bad news*.

Ludwig Oh yes, of course. *(gets out 'speech')* I shall need a chair to stand on.

Buckles Landlord ... a chair for his majesty.

Herr Pump Certainly. *(bawling)* Frankie!

Frankie *(entering)* Hello, boys and girls.

Audience Hello, Frankie.

Herr Pump Don't stand there chatting. A *chair* for Prince Ludwig.

Frankie Oh yes ... *(loudly)* Hip Hip.

All Hooray!

SONG D

Principals and Chorus

(At the end of the number, BUCKLES gets a chair and places it centre and LUDWIG stands on it)

Buckles Silence please. *(bellowing)* Quiet! Give the man a chance!

Ludwig *(clears throat and reads)* "Loyal Subjects, Citizens of Bavaria, lend me your ears."

Herr Pump Why does he want to borrow our ears?

Buckles Shshsh!

Ludwig I come to bear bad tidings not give good ones!
The evil in the night is after us
And goodness will vanish with the sun!

Frankie Get to the point!

Buckles What his highness is trying to say is ...

Ludwig There's been terrible trouble at my chateau.

Herr Pump What is it?

Ludwig Well, it's a sort of castle with turrets and a drawbridge and ...

Herr Pump No ... what's the trouble?

Ludwig Count Dracula is back!

All Dracula!

(A sinister fanfare. ALL gasp in horror and clutch their throats. PRINCE LUDWIG climbs down and BUCKLES removes the chair)

Ludwig He arrived last night with his hideous grandmother.

Herr Pump Dracula's bad enough ...

Frau Pump But Granula's even worse.

Frankie Yes, she's a pain in the neck! *(laughs)*

Ludwig *(dramatically)* They have no power while the sun is shining, but when it's dark ... beware!

(The CHORUS panic and dash for the main door. HERR and FRAU PUMPERNICKEL rush to the reception desk, pull out a suitcase and throw items into it)

Chorus *(variously)* Dracula's back! Out of my way! Wait for me! Mummy! I'm too young to die! Help! Etc. *(together as they exit)*

Frau Pump Run for your lives!

Herr Pump Let's get out of here!

Ludwig What are you doing?

Herr Pump Running away, of course! *(to audience)* And so will you if you've got any sense!

Frau Pump Yes ... Count Dracula's crazy for pretty, young girls.

Frankie You'll be quite safe then!

Frau Pump Cheek! *(moving away)* Come along, Titus.

Herr Pump Yes, dear. *(to FRANKIE)* You can send us a letter when the coast is clear.

Frau Pump If you're still alive!

Ludwig Wait!

Both No fear!

Frau Pump We're going where it's safe to walk the streets at night!

Herr Pump Where the sun shines all year round!

Ludwig Where's that?

Both *Local 'rough' area. (They exit)*

Heidi They've gone. What are we going to do?

Buckles Keep calm. That's the important thing.

Ludwig Yes. Whatever you do ... don't panic.

(There is a loud explosion: the LAB door bursts open and smoke billows onto the stage. LUDWIG and BUCKLES panic: they run in opposite directions, return and barge into each other. FRANKIE and HEIDI watch them, unruffled)

Both *(variously)* Arrgh! It's Dracula! It's Granula! Which way out? This way! No, it's this way!

(PROFESSOR CRACKPOT appears, coughing and spluttering, with his lab-coat in charred tatters. His hand raised, with the thumb and forefinger forming a "circle")

Crackpot Eureka!

Ludwig Don't worry, Heidi ... I'll protect you! *(shields her)*

Crackpot *(coming D.S.)* I've done it!

Ludwig Get back, you fiend!

Heidi It's alright, your highness.

Frankie It's just Professor Crackpot.

Crackpot Success at last! I've done it!

Ludwig Done what?

Crackpot *(showing 'circle')* Here, see! *(proudly)* My latest invention!

Heidi I can't see anything!

Crackpot That's elementary, my dear Heidi ... of course you cannot see nothing! This is a *hole*!

Others A hole??

Crackpot Ja, ja! All I need to do now is work out how to put the mint around it!

Frankie Very good, Professor ... that'll make lots of money.
Crackpot Ja, it'll make a mint! *(ALL groan)*
Heidi *(to LUDWIG)* Your Highness ...
Ludwig *(interrupting)* Ludwig.
Heidi Ludwig ... may I introduce Professor Jacob Crackpot, the most famous member of the Cracker Family.
Crackpot Ja, I am Jacob ... the cream of the Crackers.
Ludwig *(holding out hand)* How do you do ... I'm Prince Ludwig.
Crackpot *(shaking hand)* How do you do? *(letting go and scrabbling on floor)* Oh dear, oh dear, oh dear.
Ludwig What's wrong?
Crackpot I've dropped it! Ah, here it is. *(stands up holding "circle" carefully)* I'll put it in here for safe keeping. *(puts hand in pocket)* Now I've got a hole in the pocket!
Frankie More like a hole in the head!
Crackpot Maybe I could interest you in one of my latest inventions, Prince Bigwig? *(pulls a black-painted light bulb out of his pocket)*
Ludwig A black lightbulb? What use is that?
Crackpot It's very good for reading in the dark. No? *(putting bulb back in pocket)* Oh well. *(extracting a tea-bag from his pocket)* How about this then?
Ludwig What is it?
Crackpot The world's first waterproof teabag! No? *(tosses teabag over shoulder)* Then maybe I could interest you in my marvellous new invention for looking through solid walls! I call it a "window". And I have also discovered something that does the work of ten men!
Ludwig What's that?
Crackpot Ten women!
Buckles He's crazy!
Crackpot How dare you? I am the man who gave the world colour radio!
Buckles He's mad!
Crackpot I'll show you who's mad. Take a look at this! *(He rips open his lab coat. ALL recoil and cover their eyes. CRACKPOT takes a strange-looking gun from its holster)* Stick 'em up, cowboy! *(ALL step back)*
Ludwig & Buckles *(raising arms)* Don't shoot!
Frankie *(raising arms)* Careful with that thing!
Crackpot *(chuckling)* It's alright ... it's not loaded. This is my latest invention. I call it a "Hypno-Gun".
Ludwig What does it do?
Crackpot You aim it at someone. Fire it. And "hey presto" ... they are instantly hypnotised. Allow me to demonstrate. Which of you would like to volunteer? *(pointing gun at BUCKLES)*
Buckles *(stepping back)* Not likely!
(He points the gun at HEIDI and FRANKIE)

Both Keep away!

Crackpot *(pointing gun at LUDWIG)* It won't hurt a bit, I promise. Ready?

Ludwig This is ridiculous!

Crackpot Aim!

Ludwig It won't work!

Crackpot Fire! *(electronic beeping)*

Ludwig I've never been ... *(he freezes, mouth open, eyes wide)*

Frankie It's worked!

Heidi Amazing! *(she walks around LUDWIG, examining him)*

Crackpot Shsh! *(to audience)* He is now in a deep hypnotic trance, so everybody must keep very quiet. *(to LUDWIG)* Can you hear me? Nod your head if you understand. *(LUDWIG nods head)* Good! Arms up! Arms down! Touch your toes! *(LUDWIG obeys)* Excellent. Now, Heidi ... give me the first word that comes into your head!

Heidi *(behind LUDWIG)* Er ... "bottom".

Crackpot Bottom? *(HEIDI looks embarrassed)* That'll do, I suppose. *(to LUDWIG)* Listen carefully Prince Earwig. Everytime you hear the word "bottom" you will shout "knickers" at the top of your voice. Nod your head if you understand. *(LUDWIG nods)* Good. Now, I am going to count to three and snap my fingers and you will awake with no recollection of what I have just said. One. Two. Three. *(snaps fingers and LUDWIG 'awakes')*

Ludwig ... in hypnotism. I've never been hypnotised in my life. It's a load of rubbish.

Crackpot Rubbish, is it? Tell me Frankie ... if the attic's at the top of the house, where is the cellar?

Frankie *(pointing down)* Down below.

Crackpot No, no. *(whispers in his ear)*

Frankie *(giggles)* I see, Professor. If the attic's at the top of the house, the cellar's at the bottom.

Ludwig *(straightening up)* Knickers! *(Laughter. He looks confused)* What's everyone laughing at?

Crackpot Nothing. *(they laugh again)*

Ludwig I don't see what's so funny. There's nothing to laugh about. *(moves to Main Door)* We are all in grave danger. *(opens door ... a ruddy light floods in)*

Crackpot Danger?

Ludwig It's almost dark outside.

Heidi Yes. What a beautiful sunset. *(shyly)* It's so romantic.

Ludwig It's horrible!

Heidi Horrible?

Ludwig You know what they say. "Red sky at night, vampire's delight"! *(closes door)*

Crackpot Vampires? *(knowingly)* Ahhh ...

Heidi What are we going to do?

Ludwig There's only one thing to do: eat lots of garlic. *(the others grimace)* That'll drive the vampires away.

Frankie That'll drive the audience away!

Heidi There must be something else we could eat.

Crackpot Rubbish!

Frankie No, I don't fancy eating that!

Crackpot There's something that vampires hate worse than garlic.

Others What's that? *(Bubbling noises from the LAB)*

Crackpot I, Professor Crackpot, the world's greatest inventor and vampire vanquisher, have the solution. *(produces "hole" from his pocket)*

Ludwig What solution?

Crackpot My peppermint solution: I left it boiling in my laboratory.

Others Peppermint?

Ludwig You don't mean that, surely?

Crackpot I do. And don't call me "Shirley". You know what they say: "Suck a peppermint all night long 'coz vampires can't abide the pong"! *(goes the LAB door)* Come, Prince Fuzzywig. I shall need your help. *(Exits. BUCKLES moves to LAB door)*

Ludwig Coming. *(to HEIDI and FRANKIE)* Make sure that all the doors and windows are locked. *(moves to LAB)*

Frankie Yes, your Magnificence!

Heidi *(to FRANKIE)* I'll check upstairs and you check down. *(she moves to stairs)*

Frankie Right. We'll check the place from top to bottom.

Ludwig Knickers!

(The others laugh. Exit LUDWIG and BUCKLES into the LAB. FRANKIE mimes walking downstairs and disappears behind the Reception Desk. HEIDI exit upstairs.

Almost immediately, there is a loud knocking at the main door. Enter MISS NELLY. She is dressed in a travelling cloak and a mortarboard and is clutching a phrase-book)

Miss Nelly Yoo-hoo! Hello there! Anyone home? *(reading sign above the door)* "Nickelpumper's Taverna" ... well this looks like the right place! *(calling through the doors)* Alright girls, you can come in.

(Loud cheering and screeching. MISS NELLY is thrust aside as the stage is invaded by the SCHOOLGIRLS dressed in dishevelled school uniforms and battered hats. They carry bags, violin cases and hockey sticks. Members of the Chorus can be used to swell their ranks, but there are five main girls. BRIDGET is dressed 'sexily' and carries a make-up bag; MABEL is extremely dirty: she wears a scruffy cardigan and is constantly chewing gum and blowing bubbles; AGNES is a bully and a talented confidence-trickster; CONSTANCE is a swot and 'teacher's pet': she wears spectacles and always has her nose in a book; ETHEL is a hypochondriac and a constant moaner.

The unruly bunch of girls dash D.C. and sing the "School Anthem" defiantly at the audience. MISS NELLY follows and conducts the girls energetically)

SONG E

The School Anthem

"The Liberty Bell" by Sousa ("Monty Python" theme)

Don't be a dope and sit and mope
And throw you life away!
Don't go on strike: get on your bike
And just live for today!
Don't be all meek and stand for cheek:

Let nothing in your way!
Don't be polite and ladylike
And always run away!
Oh, give 'em a knuckle sandwich
On the chin!
You've gotta fight with all your might
And not give in!
When ever you're in trouble
Knock 'em out of sight!
In our school the golden rule
Is fight, fight, fight!

Miss Nelly *(during the song)* Sing out Ethel. Keep the beat Agnes. Smile Bridget. Keep going.

(The song ends. CONSTANCE steps away from the group, sits on the floor and opens her book)

Miss Nelly *(ecstatically)* When I hear your innocent little voices raised in song it makes me want to throw caution to the wind ... *(coarsely)* and belt you all in the mouth with a wet kipper! How many more times have I got to tell you to sing out?

Agnes I *did* sing out ... my voice filled the auditorium.

Miss Nelly Yes, Agnes ... half the audience left to make room for it!

Bridget Everyone knows that I'm the best singer ... I've been singing ever since I was two years old.

Miss Nelly No wonder your voice is hoarse!

(BRIDGET steps huffily away from the others and touches up her makeup)

Miss Nelly And Mabel ... you should open your mouth and *project*.

Mabel What, like this? *(She opens her mouth wide and does a 'Tarzan' bellow)*

Miss Nelly The last time I saw a mouth like that, Willie Carson was sitting behind it! *(to ETHEL)* And I didn't hear you singing at all, Ethel.

Ethel *(moaning)* Singing makes my throat sore, Miss ... I think I'm getting the flu. I've got a temperature, Miss ... *(MISS NELLY puts a hand on her forehead)*... I feel all hot and bothered.

Miss Nelly You might be hot, dear, but you'll *never* be bothered. *(turning to MABEL who is wiping her nose on her sleeve)* And don't wipe your nose on your sleeve, Mabel ... where's your hanky?

Mabel I'm trying to keep it clean, Miss.

Miss Nelly *(pointing at BRIDGET who is looking in a mirror)* You should all copy Bridget ... what a *model* pupil.

Agnes Yes, she's all stuck-up with glue.

Bridget I always try to look my best ... you never know when a handsome prince will turn up!

Girls *(sneering)* Oooooooo!

Bridget I'm destined for great things: when I was born they fired a 21 gun salute.

Mabel What a pity they missed. *(MABEL and BRIDGET shout and scuffle)*

Miss Nelly Girls! Quieten down. Why can't you be well-behaved and studious *(pointing at CONSTANCE)* like Constance?

Agnes *(snatching CONSTANCE's book)* Teacher's pet!

Constance *(standing)* Give me back my book!

Agnes Make me!

(AGNES and CONSTANCE fight, rolling on the floor. The other girls step back and egg them on. MISS NELLY observes the fight in mock-horror for a few moments before breaking it up)

Miss Nelly *(clapping hands)* Alright girls, break it up, break it up. *(She grabs them by the ears and pulls them up)* You should be ashamed of yourselves ... that's no way for ladies to behave in public. Have you forgotten what I taught you about etiquette and elocution ... and the martial arts. How many more times do I have to tell you, Agnes ... the way to get someone down on the ground is to kick their feet from under them *(she demonstrates on AGNES who lands on her bottom)* like this! And Constance ... don't pull hair, give her a quick karate chop, like this! *(she demonstrates on CONSTANCE who is felled by the blow. The other girls cheer and applaud)* See? It's easy when you know how. *(AGNES and CONSTANCE get up)* I am in the business of knocking young heads off young shoulders.

Constance *(moaning)* Miss!

Miss Nelly What is it, my pet?

Constance She stole my book, Miss!

Miss Nelly Give it to her, Agnes.

Agnes You said it ... *(she whacks CONSTANCE over the head with the book)*

Constance Ouch! Give it back or I'll tell her what you did!

Miss Nelly *(twisting CONSTANCE's ear)* What did she do?

Constance She stole your bloomers, Miss.

(MISS NELLY pats her skirt and is shocked to find them missing)

Miss Nelly Oh my goodness! *(to AGNES, calmly)* I'm impressed, Agnes ... you're a girl of hidden talents.

Agnes Thank you, Miss.

Miss Nelly Hand them over. *(AGNES extracts a large pair of bloomers from her uniform and gives them to MISS NELLY together with the book)* And take one hundred lines ... "I must not nick knickers whilst folks is still wearing 'em".

Agnes *(poking tongue out at CONSTANCE)* Tell-tale tit! *(she joins the other girls)*

Miss Nelly *(examining book)* What's this you're reading, Constance. "The Embarrassing Moment" by Lucy Lastic! *(clutches her bloomers to bosom)* Oh ... there's no need to rub it in.

Constance *(snatching book)* I wasn't Miss ... I'm studying for my exams!

Miss Nelly Exams, my foot!

Constance You said it! *(she stamps on MISS NELLY's foot)*

Miss Nelly Ouch! Alright girls, settle down. *(crossing to Reception Desk)* I shall see about our rooms. Where is everybody? The place is deserted. *(seeing the audience)* Oh look, there's lots of people out here. *(opens phrase book)* Let me see now ... oh yes ... *(reading laboriously)* "Speak-un sie En-g-lish?" *(no response)* They must be deaf as well as foreign! What's the matter, don't you understand German? Do you speak English? Speak up, I can't hear you ... can you speak English?

Audience Yes.

Miss Nelly Well that's a relief ... my German's a bit rusty. I'm having trouble with my vowels. Thank goodness I've got this phrase book to help me. It's taught me lots of things ... like how to say "yes" in twenty seven languages! The trouble is I don't get asked very often! But it doesn't really matter ... I can speak the one language that everyone understands ... the language of LOVE! Mind you, I'm a little rusty at that too, so if anyone fancies some conversation practice, I'll see you after the show!

(She rings the bell on the reception desk. FRANKIE appears instantly behind the counter)

Frankie Ja?

Miss Nelly *(frantically thumbing through phrase book)* Hang on a minute, I've lost my place. *(FRANKIE folds his arms)* Here it is ... "Have-un sie ein room-un for die night-un?"

Frankie With or without a bath?

Miss Nelly Oh, you speak English.

Frankie Ja!

Miss Nelly Ja? What terrible journey we've had!

Frankie Ja?

Miss Nelly Ja! We came by coach ... I wouldn't say it was crowded, but even the driver was standing!

Frankie Ja?

Miss Nelly Ja! It took us six days to get here ... four days on the coach and two days to fold the map.

Frankie Ja?

Miss Nelly Ja! Is that all you can say?

Frankie Ja!

Miss Nelly Are you the landlord?

Frankie Nein, nein, Fraulein ... I'm Frank N. Stein.

Miss Nelly *(stepping back, horrified)* Arrgh! It's Frankenstein! Get him, girls!

(The GIRLS attack him. Enter HEIDI from upstairs)

Frankie Ouch! No! Call them off!

Heidi What's going on here?

Miss Nelly Heel, girls.

(The GIRLS stand back. A ripping noise as FRANKIE staggers to his feet. AGNES holds up a pair of underpants)

Agnes Got 'em! *(the GIRLS cheer)*

Frankie Are you deaf, or what? I said "my name is Frank N. Stein".

Miss Nelly What does the "N" stand for?

Frankie Neil.

Miss Nelly *(kneeling)* If you insist. *(offering hand)* How do you do, Mr. Stein.

Heidi He's not a "Mr" ... he's a "Herr".

Agnes *(displaying underpants)* He doesn't look like a "her" to me.

Miss Nelly *(standing)* Agnes Swipe! You give those back to Mr. Stein. *(FRANKIE clutches himself incredulously)*

Agnes Awww, Miss ... I want them for my collection, Miss.

Miss Nelly At once!

Agnes Yes, Miss.

(She returns them to FRANKIE who turns his back on the audience and stuffs them down his trousers. BRIDGET examines HEIDI contemptuously)

Heidi I hope your girls are going to behave themselves.

Miss Nelly Oh yes ... my girls are proper little madams. *(BRIDGET tugs HEIDI's hair)*

Heidi Ow! We're in enough trouble as it is. *(moves to Reception Desk. MABEL trips her up)*

Miss Nelly *(dignified)* My girls are the crumb de la crumb. *(The GIRLS cheer and jeer. HEIDI retreats behind the Reception Desk)*

Miss Nelly Now then, have you got our rooms ready? *(HEIDI shakes her head)* I booked them by telephone.

Heidi That's impossible: telephones haven't been invented yet.

Miss Nelly But I've got reservations! *(aside)* and I should have by the look of this dump!

Heidi *(producing a large, dusty ledger)* What name is it please?

Miss Nelly Let's see ... there's Mable Crumb, Ethel Ready, Agnes Swipe, Bridget Bloggs ...

Heidi Nein. Nein.

Miss Nelly *(counting girls)* Oh, there's more than nine of us.

Heidi No. What's *your* name?

Miss Nelly "Nelly".

Heidi 'Mrs' or 'Miss'

Miss Nelly 'Miss' *(nudging FRANKIE)* ... but you never know your luck.

Heidi *(writing)* Miss Smelly.

Miss Nelly 'Nelly'! 'Nelly'!

Frankie Oh ... as in 'elephant'.

Miss Nelly Watch it, buster.

Heidi *(writing)* Smelly Nelly ...

Miss Nelly *(exasperated)* No ... the name is **Miss Nelly**.

Girls *('Singing' the "Dallas Theme")* Tra la, la la ... etc *(MISS NELLY conducts them for a few seconds and then signals them to stop)*

Frankie That's a stupid name!

Miss Nelly How dare you! I'm very well educated: my full title is Miss Nelly B.A., Ph.D., M.Sc., and Iceberg.

Frankie Iceberg?

Miss Nelly Yes, I've got 'lettuce' after my name! *(producing passport from bag)* Here's my passport if you don't believe me. *(FRANKIE opens it and laughs)* What are you laughing at?

Frankie You look even worse than your passport photograph.

Miss Nelly That photo doesn't do me justice.

Frankie It's mercy you want, not justice. And look at this ... you've crossed out your date of birth.
Miss Nelly *(snatching passport back)* I don't want people to know how old I am.
Frankie Yes. Few women admit their age.
Miss Nelly And few men act theirs! Eh, girls? *(GIRLS cheer and shake their fists. To audience)* This is a feminist panto. *(to HEIDI)* Now what about our rooms?
Heidi *(shaking head)* I'm sorry, there's too many of you.
Miss Nelly But you don't expect us to find another hotel at this time of night, surely?
Heidi My name's "Heidi".
Miss Nelly Sorry. You must be able to squash us in somewhere, Heidi ... try!
All Ho-di-ho!
Heidi Well, you can have my room if you like. I'll sleep down here.
Miss Nelly How kind.
Heidi That's settled then. Would you like morning tea in your chamber?
Miss Nelly I'd prefer it in a cup.
Heidi *(offering ledger)* Sign here please.
Miss Nelly Where?
Heidi At the **bottom**.
Ludwig *(throwing open LAB door)* Knickers! *(slams door)*
(MISS NELLY comes to edge of stage, outraged. The SCHOOLGIRLS step forward and scan the audience threateningly)
Miss Nelly How rude! Who said that? Who was it? Own up! *(pointing at someone in the front row)* It was you, wasn't it? *(rolling up sleeves)* I'm going to come down there and give you a good hiding.
Frankie It wasn't his fault.
Heidi No. It was Ludwig.
Miss Nelly Oh, it was Ludwig, was it? I'll knock his block off!
Frankie You can't do that.
Miss Nelly Why not?
Heidi He's a prince!
Girls A prince!
Bridget *(excited)* Is there a prince staying here?
Heidi *(defensive)* Yes. He's a good friend of mine, actually.
Bridget I'm *dying* to meet him! Where is he?
Frankie He's in the lab.
Miss Nelly In the **lav**? *(covers her mouth in "horror")*
(The LAB door opens. Enter BUCKLES)
Frankie Here he comes now.
Buckles Make way for his royal Highness, Prince Ludwig of Bavaria. *(Enter LUDWIG)*
Girls *(sighing)* He's gorgeous!
Miss Nelly Attention! *(the GIRLS line up)* Let's give his highness a right royal salute. *(saluting)* Dib dib dib.
Girls *(saluting)* Dub dub dub.
Miss Nelly *(shaking fist)* Oompah. Oompah.

Girls *(shaking fist)* Stick it up your jumper! *(the GIRLS cheer and MISS NELLY curtsies)*

Ludwig *(to FRANKIE, annoyed)* Where did this lot come from?

Miss Nelly *(rising)* That's charming, that is!

Ludwig And who are you?

Miss Nelly They call me ... **Miss Nelly!**

(The girls sing the "Dallas Theme". MISS NELLY conducts and then signals them to stop. The GIRLS surround LUDWIG)

Agnes Are you real prince, or just a pretendy one?

Ludwig Of course I'm real ... I'm first in line for the throne.

Ethel In that case, I'm glad I went before I came!

Bridget *(shoving the others aside)* My name's Bridget. But you can call me "Brigitte". *(curtseys)*

Ludwig Ah, mais oui!

Bridget Any time! *(She takes his arm and rests her head on his shoulder. HEIDI looks mortified)* I love princes. They're so rich and handsome.

Constance *(tugging his sleeve)* Can we come and visit your palace?

Ludwig I haven't got a palace. *(BRIDGET looks disappointed and lets go)* I live in a chateau. It's in the middle of the Black Forest.

Miss Nelly *(to audience)* How delicious. A Black Forest Chateau!

Ludwig *(breaking away from GIRLS)* This is terrible!

Miss Nelly It wasn't that bad!

Ludwig These girls are far too attractive. *(GIRLS simper)* They'll have to go!

Ethel But I don't need to go right now.

Ludwig Avaunt! Be gone! Before it's too late!

Miss Nelly What for?

Ludwig You know what they say ... "Many maidens maketh a magnet for malevolence".

Miss Nelly Try saying that again with your teeth in.

Ludwig "Many maidens maketh ..."

Miss Nelly Don't bother. *(to FRANKIE)* What's he on about?

Frankie Dracula!

Girls *(clutching throats)* Dracula! *(a sinister fanfare)*

Miss Nelly What are we going to do?

Frankie Munch a mint and breath heavily. *(blows)*

Heidi Vampires hate the smell of peppermint.

Buckles Everyone knows that.

Ludwig There's only one problem.

Miss Nelly What's that?

Ludwig Peppermints haven't been invented yet!

(There is an explosion. The LAB door bursts ope[illegible] RACKPOT appears)

Crackpot Eureka! At last!

Ludwig You've done it?

Crackpot Ja and nein. You want the good news or the bad news?

Ludwig The good news.

Crackpot The good news is ... I have invented the world's first peppermint!

All Hooray!

Frankie Wait. *(to CRACKPOT)* What's the bad news?

(CRACKPOT produces a giant "Polo" mint. Groans all round. FRANKIE takes the mint)

Crackpot Oh well, back to the laboratory! *(slams LAB door)*

Frankie Now what are we going to do?

Miss Nelly Even Mabel couldn't get her gob round that.

(There is a crash of thunder and a flash of lightning)

Frankie That sounds like trouble!

Ludwig Are all the doors and windows locked?

Heidi *(pointing up)* Everything's locked upstairs.

Frankie *(pointing down)* And everything's locked downstairs.

Heidi And everything's locked ... Oh no!

Ludwig What is it?

Heidi We forgot to lock the **front door**.

(A loud crash of thunder and a flash of lightning. The lights dim and the Main Door is thrown open. DRACULA stands silhouetted in the doorway. ALL shriek and move left and right, leaving centre-stage clear. DRACULA spreads his cloak and flaps his way to C., laughing horribly)

Ludwig *(stepping forward)* Get back, you fiend!

Dracula *(extra posh lisp)* Oh, be a sport, old chap!

Ludwig What do you want with us?

Dracula I'm a bit thirsty, actually ... *(he chortles)* I want to wet the old whistle! *(sinisterly)* I need a drink of blood!

Frankie We only serve beer here!

Dracula Oh come, come, come ... why the place is simply brimming with maidens ... surely you can spare me one or two. *(he moves towards GIRLS who raise their hockey sticks and jeer)* On second thoughts, this lot looks a bit tough. *(he chortles, moves suddenly and grabs HEIDI)* But you look pretty tasty, my dear.

Heidi Let go of me, you monster!

Dracula You and I could make beautiful music together!

Heidi What kind of music?

Dracula The death march!

(He sings and forces HEIDI to dance. AGNES sneaks up behind him)

Dracula Heaven! You're in Heaven!
And your heart beats so you can't keep it in check:
So just give in and whisper "what the heck!"
When we're out together, dancing, tooth to neck!

(A ripping noise. AGNES triumphantly waves a pair of black 'Y'-fronts. The GIRLS cheer. DRACULA lets go of HEIDI and crosses his legs)

Heidi *(to audience)* Help! Help!

Ludwig *(to audience)* Quickly, everyone whistle for Kodak.

(ALL whistle. KODAK bounds onstage, and bites DRACULA's bottom. He lets go of HEIDI who runs into PRINCE LUDWIG's arms)

Dracula Arrgh! A doggy! I hate doggies! Get that mutt away from me! *(FRANKIE puts the giant mint over DRACULA's head)* Arrgh! Peppermint. Curses! *(wheezing)* Fools! Fools! Nincompoops! I'll be back!

Frankie *(encouraging audience)* Booo!

All Booo!

(Exit DRACULA. ALL cheer)

Ludwig Quickly, everybody ... barricade the door so he can't get back in.

(The SCHOOLGIRLS and BUCKLES move furniture up against the Main Door)

Heidi What are we going to do?

Frankie How are we going to get rid of him?

Ludwig Wait until the sun comes up tomorrow, then we'll be safe. Vampires hate the sunshine!

SONG F
Ensemble

End of Scene 1

Act One
Scene 2
Outside Pumpernickel's Taverna - night

(Enter GRANULA D.R. supporting herself on a walking stick. She looks old and frail but is actually agile and wilful)

Granula *(calling sweetly)* Dracula! Dracula! *(harshly)* Where has that good-for-nothing got to? *(calling sweetly)* Dracky-baby! Where are you?

(Enter DRACULA D.L., staggering)

Dracula Help! It got me, Granny!

Granula What got you?

Dracula A doggy. It bit me.

Granula Where?

Dracula *(rubbing bottom)* Here!

Granula On your **bottom**?

Ludwig *(appearing)* Knickers! *(disappears)*

Granula *(hitting DRACULA)* Don't be so cheeky!

Dracula I didn't say anything. *(drops to knees)* Oh, I feel ever so icky! *(coughs and wheezes)*

Granula *(pointing at "Polo")* What's that? *(sniffing)* Pooh! Peppermint! *(holds nose, removes the mint and rolls it offstage)* You big twit. Have you forgotten everything I taught you? Repeat after me ... "Peppermint ..."

Dracula *(reciting)* If there's peppermint about: stick a clothes peg on your snout!

Granula Good. *(sticks a clothes peg on his nose)*

Dracula *(nasally)* Every bone in my body hurts.

Granula Just be thankful you're not a kipper! There's only one cure for peppermint-poisoning.

Dracula Wat's dat?

Granula Bat kisses! *(she whistles)* Where's my little bats? *(whistles again)* Come along, come to granny! *(Enter junior dancers, dressed as BATS)* That's nice. *(patting one of them)* Coochee, coochee, coo! *(to audience)* Aren't they disgusting? *(claps hands)* Attention! Now ...
Flap your wings and squeak and prance
Gnash your fangs and do your dance!

DANCE A
The Bat Dance

Granula *(clapping)* Well done! Excellent! Now be good little bats and give Uncle Dracky a big sloppy kiss!

(The BATS "fly" past DRACULA and blow him kisses before exiting. DRACULA revives and stands)

Dracula That's better. *(removes peg and clutches stomach)* Oh, tummy's rumbling! I haven't had a bite all night. If I don't get a drink of blood soon my mouth will heal up!

Granula *(indicating audience)* Well, what about this lot? They look nice and juicy.

Dracula *(peering at audience)* Oh, I say! Boys and girls! Postively scrumptious!

Granula Let me get my false fangs in and we'll have a feast. *(Produces a pair of 'false fangs'. To audience)* You don't mind if we come down and have a bite, do you? *('clacks' fangs)*

Audience Yes!

(Enter KODAK D.L., unnoticed by the other two. He sniffs around at edge of stage)

Dracula Spoil sports!

Granula Don't worry, kiddies ... one little nip from my gnashers and it'll all be over ... ha ha! Come on, I'm starving. Let's chew the children.

Dracula Yes. We'll bite the boys and guzzle the girls.

Granula Count to ten and we'll fly down there and chomp them all to pieces!

Dracula Spiffing! *(moves to side of stage near KODAK)*

Granula Ready?

Dracula O.K. yah!

Granula Prepare for take-off. *(they spread their cloaks and make engine noises)* Brrrrm. One ...

(As she counts, KODAK comes across the stage and sniffs at DRACULA's leg. DRACULA wraps his 'wings' around himself and watches the dog fearfully. KODAK walks around him and sniffs at the other leg)

Granula ... eight ... nine ... ten!

(KODAK cocks his leg on DRACULA)

Dracula *(wailing)* Waaah!

Granula What's wrong now!

Dracula *(shaking leg)* That doggy just attacked me!

Granula Idiot! *(crossing to KODAK)* You're not frightened of that mangey mongrel, are you? *(DRACULA nods. She approaches KODAK)* Well I'm not! Out of my way, flea-brain! *(KODAK growls ferociously and she jumps back)* Arrgh! Poisonous pooch! He's protecting them! You may have escaped this time ... but we'll be back!

Audience Booo!

Granula Shut yer gobs!

Dracula There's plenty more juicy necks inside the hotel.

Granula All we need is one open window. Come on, let's fly.

(They spread their cloaks and make engine noises. KODAK barks and chases them to the edge of the stage. Exit GRANULA and DRACULA, flapping. KODAK whines, looks skywards and remains onstage as the tabs open on the next scene)

End of Scene 2

Act One
Scene 3
The Haunted Bedroom

(A window and moonlit exterior. A bed, with "Heidi" painted on the headboard and room to hide underneath. BRIDGET's bag lies open on the bed. A bedside table with a lit candle. A trunk with a false back set against the wall. Five sleeping bags.
BRIDGET is sitting on the bed brushing her hair in a hand-mirror and singing "Keep Young and Beautiful". She is wearing a nightdress and fluffy slippers. The other girls are also wearing nightdresses and are lying in their sleeping bags on the floor. AGNES is still wearing her battered school hat, shoes and socks. CONSTANCE is reading a book.
(As BRIDGET sings, a bat flutters outside the window. AGNES, MABEL and ETHEL block their ears and howl like dogs. "Outside", KODAK cocks his ears and listens)

Bridget Don't you like my singing?
Others No!
Agnes You're driving us bats!
(Squeaking. The bat flutters against the window)
Bridget What's that?
Agnes *(getting up)* I said "You're driving us bats"!
Bridget I heard a noise. Listen! *(The bat disappears as she turns to look out of the window. KODAK barks)*
Agnes It's just a dog.
Bridget Give me your shoe.
Agnes *(removing shoe)* What for?
Bridget 'Coz I don't want to be kept awake all night long. *(takes shoe and holds nose)* Pooh! *(opens window)* Ready, aim, fire!
(She throws the shoe out of window. Swannee whistle. She leans out, watching it descend. KODAK continues barking. A shoe drops on him from above. He whimpers and exits)
Bridget *(pulling head inside)* Bullseye! *(excitedly)* Oooo ... look!
(ETHEL and MABEL get up and join them)
Ethel *(getting up)* What is it?
Bridget The view! Isn't it spectacular? Look, there's the Matterhorn.
Constance *(looking up from her book)* The Matterhorn's in Switzerland, stupid.
Ethel Yes. That's the Matterlove.
Mabel What's the "Matterlove"?
Ethel Nothing, what's wrong with you? *(they laugh)*
Bridget *(sighing and leaning on the window sill)* Moonlight on the mountains. It's so romantic. If only Ludwig was here.
Constance You'd better shut that window!
Bridget What for? *(looks out)*
Constance Vampires! That's what for.
Bridget *(looks down)* They can't get in here. We're too high up.
Constance Vampires can fly, idiot! It says so in this book.

Bridget There's nobody here. *(calling)* Hello! *(to CONSTANCE)* See? I told you so.
Echo Hello ...
Bridget *(moving away from window)* Arrgh! It's Dracula.
Agnes Don't be daft. It's only an echo. Listen. *(calling)* Yodel-ay-ee-oo!
Echo Yodel-ay-ee-oo ...
Ethel Brilliant! *(pushing AGNES aside)* Let me have a shot. *(calling)* Yoo-hoo!
Echo Yoo-hoo ...
Mabel *(pushing ETHEL aside)* My turn. *(calling)* Bridget stinks!
Echo Bridget stinks ...
(They laugh. BRIDGET shoves her aside)
Bridget Out of my way. I'll do it. *(calling)* I'm so beautiful! *(looks in mirror and preens)*
Echo You're so ugly ...
(BRIDGET is mortified and slams the window shut. The others laugh)
Ethel Truth will out!
Bridget *(moving to bed)* Huh! The last time I was in Germany, I was taken for Samantha Fox.
Agnes But they soon brought you back again! *(BRIDGET returns the mirror to the bag and takes a bottle of perfume)* What's that stuff?
Bridget This is exclusive French toilet-water. It costs £20 a bottle!
Ethel £20 for toilet-water!
Mabel Come to my house and you can have it for free!
Bridget It's delicious! *(holding up bottle)* "Midnight in Paris". *(sprays perfume)*
Ethel Smells more like low-tide at... *(local seaside resort)*! Pooh! *(holds nose)*
Bridget I'm going to turn Prince Ludwig's head.
Agnes More likely his stomach!
Bridget *(holding out hand to imaginary figure and curtseying)* Oh yes, your highness. I do! I do! I do!
Ethel What are you "doing", Bridget?
Bridget I'm practising for when Prince Ludwig asks for my hand in marriage, of course.
Mabel You'll be lucky! He's only got eyes for Heidi.
Bridget She doesn't stand a chance now I'm around.
Miss Nelly *(voice off)* Yoo-hoo!
Agnes *(going to door)* Shshsh!
Miss Nelly *(voice off)* Hello, girls!
Agnes It's Miss Nelly. *(giggling)* Come on, let's play a trick on her. *(takes pillows from the bed)*
Mabel What sort of trick?
Agnes A horrible one! *(stuffs pillows into the sleeping bag)* We'll hide and jump out at her!
Ethel Oh yes! *(helps AGNES)*
Mabel She'll have a heart attack! *(they look for hiding places)*
Bridget We'll pretend to be asleep. *(gets into sleeping bag)*
Miss Nelly *(voice off)* Yoo hoo, girls. Where are you?
Constance Hurry. Here she comes.

(BRIDGET and CONSTANCE lie down and snore loudly. ETHEL jumps into the bed and pulls the sheet over her. AGNES hides under the bed. MABEL gets into the trunk. Enter MISS NELLY breathlessly)

Miss Nelly *(to audience)* Phew! What a lot of stairs. I'm pooped. *(clapping hands)* Come along girls, it's time for beddy-byes! *(CONSTANCE and BRIDGET snore louder)* They're fast asleep already. That's not like them! *(MISS NELLY stretches and yawns)* Still, it's been a long day. I'm tired out as well. *(scratching)* I'd better get my nightie on and hit the sack.

(She starts to undo clothing. BRIDGET and CONSTANCE sit up and the others peep out from their hiding-places. They wolf-whistle)

Agnes Get 'em off!

(They duck out of sight. MISS NELLY gasps and accuses someone in the audience)

Miss Nelly Oh! Don't you be so cheeky! *(to the whole audience)* And what are all you lot staring at? *(coy)* Don't you know it's rude to watch a young lady undress? Cover your eyes immediately. Come on ... put your hands over your eyes, like this ... *(she demonstrates)*. Everybody! *(audience puts hands over eyes)* That's better. And no peeping!

(Music: "The Stripper". MISS NELLY performs a frenetic striptease with a seemingly impossible number of layers and ending with outrageous underwear. She disappears offstage and returns instantly in a nightdress: this quick change is achieved by slitting the nightdress up the back and using a velcroed fastening at the top. Assistants off-stage hold the nightdress open so that she can 'walk' into it.

The various layers could follow a theme, for example:

1. Skirts with messages such as: "Keep Out", "Handle With Care", "Do Not Bend", "Don't Open Till Christmas", "This Side Up", "Fragile", "Via Air Mail", "Top Secret".

2. A layer of "flags of the world" or laundry on a line which she hooks onto the bedpost, winding herself out.

The striptease finishes. MISS NELLY sits on the end of the bed)

Miss Nelly Now for some shut-eye. *(looking at feet)* Oh, what am I doing! I can't go to bed with my shoes on, can I? I'd better take them off. *(AGNES thrusts a leg out between hers. She removes one shoe)* That's one foot. *(removes other shoe)* That's two feet. *(removes shoe from AGNES' foot)* That's three feet! *(double take)* Three feet? *(AGNES pulls foot back in. MISS NELLY counts)* One. Two. I must be seeing things. Now for the socks! *(AGNES puts foot out again. MISS NELLY removes socks)* That's one foot. That's two feet. That's three feet! Arrgh! *(She stands. AGNES withdraws foot. To audience)* I'm going off my rocker. Did you see something?

Audience Yes.

Miss Nelly Is there somebody under the bed?

Audience Yes.

Miss Nelly *(clutching herself fearfully)* Oh my goodness! What if it's a big, strong, hairy man! *(to audience)* Is there a man under the bed?

Audience No!

Miss Nelly *(disappointed)* That's a pity. Are you sure there's someone under there?

Audience Yes.

Miss Nelly I'd better take a look then. *(kneels down, reaches under the bed and feels around)* No. There's nobody under here. *(stops groping and straightens up)* You must be imagining things. You've all gone potty! *(AGNES holds a potty out from under the bed. MISS NELLY takes it)* Oh, thank you. *(double-take)* Huh? There's something fishy going on here and I'm going to get to the **bottom** of it! *(peers under bed)*

Ludwig *(appearing instantly)* Knickers! *(disappears again)*

(MISS NELLY stands and approaches the audience, outraged)

Miss Nelly How dare you!! Who said that? Come on, own up ... who was it? Nobody, as usual. *(picks clothes up)* The riff-raff they let in here on a *(current day)* night. Disgusting! I'll just pick these clothes up and then I can get to bed. *(opens lid of trunk, tosses garments inside, and closes lid. Returns to bed)* There, that's that! *(The trunk opens and the clothes are thrown out. Swannee whistle. She picks up shoes and socks)* Oh dear, I forgot my shoes and socks. *(returns to trunk)* Must keep the place tidy. *(sees pile on floor)* Oh! Where did this lot come from? I could have sworn I put them in the trunk! *(opens lid and puts clothes, shoes and socks inside and slams it again)* There. All done. *(The lid opens and the clothes fly out again - swannee whistle. She sees it happen)* Arrgh! Did you see that? This bedroom's h-h-haunted! I'm p-p-p-petrified of sp-p-p-ooks! Where can I hide? I know ... the bed. *(She runs over to the bed. ETHEL rises up, covered by the sheet and wailing horribly)* Arrgh! A spook! Mummy! Let me out of here!

(She exits. All the GIRLS emerge and fall about laughing)

Agnes She fell for it!

Ethel Did you see her face!

Mabel She was as white as a sheet!

Miss Nelly *(returning)* You little horrors! *(to audience)* And you can stop giggling as well. It's not funny. *(to GIRLS)* How could you be so cruel? Where's your heart?

Agnes Down my throat and first on the left, Miss!

Miss Nelly *(hitting her)* That's enough of your nonsense. Get to bed. All of you. *(she crosses to the window)*

Girls Yes, Miss Nelly! *(They get into the sleeping-bags)*

Miss Nelly It's stuffy in here. I'll open the window and let in some fresh air.

Constance *(urgently)* Miss! Don't do that, Miss!

Miss Nelly Why not?

Constance Dracula and Granula might get in, Miss.

Miss Nelly *(opens window)* Don't be daft! We're right up at the top of the tavern and they're way down at the **bottom**!

Ludwig *(appearing instantly)* Knickers! *(disappears)*

Miss Nelly *(going to bed)* I don't care what you say. I can't sleep with the window shut.

Constance But, Miss. Everyone knows that vampires can fly.

Miss Nelly Rubbish.

Constance They turn themselves into bats, Miss.

Miss Nelly You're the one that's bats! *(gets into bed)*

Constance It says so in this book.

Agnes Swot!
Mabel Shut up!
Ethel Go to sleep!
(The other girls lie down)
Constance *(to audience)* Vampires *can* fly, can't they?
Audience Yes.
Miss Nelly Phooey! *(Lifts candle. "Squeaking". A bat appears at the window)*
Night night, sleep tight
And don't let the bogies bite! *(takes deep breath)*
Constance *(pointing at bat)* Miss! Miss!
Miss Nelly What is it now? *(the others sit up)*
Constance There's a bat at the window!
(The others turn to look as the bat disappears)
Miss Nelly Where? There's nothing there!
Bridget She's just trying to trick you, Miss.
Others Yes, Miss!
Constance *(to audience)* There was a bat there, wasn't there?
Audience Yes.
Miss Nelly *(to audience)* Fibbers! You're as bad as she is. Settle down and go to sleep! Nighty, nighty!
Others Pyjama, pyjama!
(The other girls lie down. MISS NELLY blows out the candle. Gloom. Snoring. Eerie music and squeaking as the bat appears at the window once more. CONSTANCE clutches her book to her and listens fearfully, without turning round. A rumble of thunder and a flash: GRANULA appears, hanging onto the window-sill. She cackles horribly as she climbs inside)
Audience Booo!
Granula Oh, shut up, you little morons! *(calling out of the window)* Dracula.
Dracula *(voice off)* Yes, Granula?
Granula Up here. I've found an open window. *("squeaking" - a bat appears outside)* And don't squeak so loud ... you'll wake our dinner up!
(A flash and DRACULA appears hanging on the window-sill)
Dracula *(slipping down)* I'm slipping! Help!
(CONSTANCE nudges the other girls awake. They sit up in their sleeping bags and clutch each other in terror. GRANULA struggles to pull DRACULA up, leaning precariously out of the window)
Constance I can hear something.
Bridget So can I.
(They stand up in their sleeping-bags)
Agnes *(to audience)* Can you see anything?
Audience Dracula!
Girls Dracula!
(They turn and see the vampires. GRANULA succeeds in tugging DRACULA through the window. He tumbles on top of her.)

Granula Arrgh! You great lump! *(The GIRLS shriek and exit, hopping in their sleeping bags)* Get off me. *(They get up. DRACULA moves to the bed)* Now look what you've done. Supper's escaped. Quickly. After them. *(moves away)*

Dracula You go. I'm fed up with schoolgirls.

Granula But they're your favourite.

Dracula Not any more. *(pointing at headboard)* Look who I've found ... "Heidi". *(chortles)* What a nice meal she'll make. *(with relish)* Heidi and chips! Heidi on toast! Heidi pie!

Miss Nelly *(sitting up)* Ho-di-ho! *(lies down and covers herself with the sheet again)*

Granula Suit yourself. All the more for me then. *(calling off)* Ready or not, here comes Granny! *(flaps her cloak and disappears)*

Dracula *(to audience)* I'm going to get Heidi this time nobody will stand in my way. *(laughs fiendishly)*

Audience Booo!

Dracula Be quiet ... *(pointing at bed)* I don't want you waking little Heidi up. *(he chortles)* At last I've got her! One quick bite and she's mine forever! Watch this! *(He holds his hands out, mesmerising the sleeping 'Heidi'. Soft, eerie music)* Heidi! Heidi! Come to me, Heidi! *(MISS NELLY sits up in bed, the sheet draped over her)* That's the way, Heidi. Now stand up, and walk over to me here. *(He beckons slowly and the music continues. MISS NELLY, still draped, walks across to him)* Stop! *(MISS NELLY stops)* Like a lamb to the slaughter! Are you ready to become the Bride of Dracula, my dear?

Miss Nelly *(high pitched)* Yes, oh master!

Dracula *(baring fangs)* Good! *(taking hold of sheet)* And now for the kiss of death! *(he pulls the sheet off)*

Miss Nelly Kissy! Kissy! *(she puckers her lips)*

Dracula Arrgh! *(he steps back)*

Miss Nelly *(hands on hips)* Come on then, I'm waiting!

Dracula Help, Granny! It's a monster! *(Exit)*

Miss Nelly *(to audience)* Cheek! Come back here! *(Exit)*

End of Scene 3

Act One
Scene 4
A Hallway in Pumpernickel's Taverna

(Enter FRANKIE wearing a nightshirt and cap)

Frankie	Hello, boys and girls.
Audience	Hello, Frankie.
Frankie	*(yawning)* I'm having a terrible job getting to sleep. I keep hearing funny noises. Creaks and squeaks and moans and groans and screams. *(screams off-stage)* There it is again! *(Enter GIRLS at opposite side, hopping in their sleeping-bags)*
Bridget	Quick.
Agnes	Faster.
Frankie	I might have known! What are you lot doing out of bed?
Bridget	*(breathlessly)* We're racing ... *(continues past him)*
Frankie	At this time of night? *(to AGNES)* Who's winning?
Agnes	No, we're racing to get away. *(continues past him)*
Frankie	Who from?
Mabel	Granula.
Ethel	She's right behind us.
Constance	Run for your life!
	(They reach the opposite side. Enter GRANULA in front of them)
Granula	Ah-ha! Gotcha! *(The GIRLS collapse in a heap)*
Frankie	*(encouraging audience)* Boo!
Audience	Boo!
Granula	Oh, be quiet. I'm not going to hurt them. *(opening cloak and bending, sweetly over the GIRLS)* I only want to give them a nice, little bedtime kiss *(to audience)* ... on the neck!
Frankie	*(to audience)* I'd better try and rescue them. *(to GRANULA)* You wouldn't hurt these poor defenceless little girls, surely?
	(The GIRLS start to crawl away and exit one by one)
Granula	I would. And don't call me "Shirley". *(displaying false fangs)* I'm going to crunch 'em and munch 'em and scrunch 'em!
Frankie	Over my dead body.
Granula	That can be arranged. *(pushes him aside)* Out of my way.
Frankie	*(detaining her)* Wait. I want to ask you something first.
Granula	What is it?
Frankie	Is that your real face or are you just on your way to a Halloween Party?
Granula	How dare you! *(stroking cheek)* I have the face of an 18 year old girl.
Frankie	Well give it back, you're getting it all wrinkled!
Granula	Are you trying to make a fool out of me?
Frankie	No, I never interfer with nature!
Granula	Enough of this nonsense. *(raising fangs)* It's maiden-munching time! *(turns)* Curses! They've got away. And it's all your fault.

Frankie You win a few, you lose a few. I'll be off then ...

Granula Stay where you are! *They* might have escaped ... but *you* haven't. *(producing false fangs)* How would you like to join my club?

Frankie What club?

Granula My **fang** club! *(clacks fangs)*

Frankie *(clutching throat)* No thanks!

Granula *(beckoning hypnotically with other hand)* Come to Granny!

Frankie *(sleep-walking)* Yes, oh ugly one!

Granula Stop! I'll just pop my fangs in.

Frankie Wait ... I've got a better idea. Why don't you give me your choppers and make me bite myself?

Granula Brilliant! Why didn't I think of that? *(gives him the teeth)* Here you are.

Frankie Ta! *(He holds them up, clacks them like castinets and sings)* "Oh this year I'm off to sunny Spain ... Y Viva Espana!"

Granula Stop larking about!

Frankie *(holding teeth like a glove puppet)* Hello, Orville, how are you today? *(impersonating ventriloquist)* "I'm thuper, Fwankie ... how are you?"

Granula Stop! *(hypnotising with hands)* I'm going to make you bite yourself!

Frankie *(encouraging audience)* Oh no you won't!

Granula Oh yes I will!

Frankie & Audience Oh no you won't! *(repeat once more)*

Granula Oh yes I will! *(stamping feet)* Will, will, will, will, will. *(hypnotising)* Just give in without a fight, and let my dentures chomp and bite!

(A drum-roll. FRANKIE tries to restrain the teeth, but his hand moves them inexorably towards his neck)

Frankie Oo-er! *(to audience)* Help me! Quick! Whistle for Kodak! *(the audience whistles)* Louder!

(Enter KODAK, growling. GRANULA shrieks and backs away. FRANKIE continues to struggle with the teeth)

Granula Curses! Curses! Foiled again. *(shaking fist at audience)* But I'll be back and next time I won't fail!

Audience Boo! *(KODAK barks and she exits)*

Frankie *(still holding the teeth at bay)* Thanks a lot everybody! Good boy, Kodak, you got here just in the **neck** of time! Ha ha. What am I laughing at? This is serious. *(struggling to control the teeth)* These dentures have got a mind of their own! I can't stop them. Ugh! *(forces the teeth to arm length and lets his free hand drop)* Phew! That's better. They almost got me. *(drum-roll ... his hand moves down towards his bottom)* Now what are they doing? What's up? No, no. Keep back. Get off! *(chases himself across the stage with the teeth)* Arrgh! Mummy! Save me! *(the teeth bite his bottom - a cymbal)* Ouch! I've bitten myself! *(sound of distant amublance siren)* Has anyone got an "Elastoplast"? Ow! Help!

(KODAK howls. The ambulance siren gets louder and stops as CRACKPOT enters, pushing a trolley)

Crackpot What's wrong?

Frankie Granula got me. I've been bitten!

Crackpot *(examining his neck)* Let me see. There might still be time to save you!

Frankie *(embarrassed)* She didn't bite me there.

Crackpot Where did she bite you?

Frankie *(coy)* I don't like to say ...

Crackpot Don't be shy.

Frankie *(loud whisper)* On the **bottom.** *(LUDWIG instantly enters, followed by HEIDI)*

Ludwig Knickers!

Frankie No, it's true. Look.

(He starts to hitch nightshirt up, realises audience is looking and faces front before continuing. CRACKPOT and LUDWIG examine him and shake their heads. HEIDI averts her face)

Crackpot That looks nasty. Did you put anything on it?

Frankie No, she seemed to like it just the way it was.

Ludwig Tut tut. You have a scar!

Frankie No thanks, I don't smoke! *(lowers nightshirt and staggers)* Oooo ... I feel woozy! *(LUDWIG help him onto the trolley)*

Heidi How is he, Professor?

Crackpot He is suffering from a bad case of vampire poisoning! We must operate at once!

Frankie *(alarmed)* Operate??

Crackpot We will cut everything off.

Frankie *(sitting up)* Everything??

Crackpot And sew it back on again!

Frankie Waah! Let me out of here! *(tries to get off the trolley but is forced back again)*

Crackpot *(holding up a giant syringe)* One little jab and it will all be over. Don't worry, this won't hurt a bit. *(injects FRANKIE)*

Frankie Arrgh! That hurt!

Crackpot I know ... I lied!

Crackpot Now go to sleep and I will turn you into a new man.

Frankie I don't want to be a new man. I just want to be Frank N. Stein!

Crackpot Don't worry. You *will* be Frankenstein!

Frankie That's alright then! *(closes eyes)*

Heidi Is he asleep, Professor?

(CRACKPOT pulls a card saying "ZZZZZZZ" from under the pillow and holds it over FRANKIE's head)

Crackpot Ja! *(covers FRANKIE with a sheet)* Quickly. To the laboratory!

(Ambulance sirens as they push the trolley off and the tabs open on Scene 5)

End of Scene 4

Act One
Scene 5
Professor Crackpot's Laboratory

(This scene uses the same basic set as Scene 1 with a few adjustments. (1) The stairs are repositioned U.R. over the "Lab" door. (2) The window is covered with a wall-chart depicting a weird mechanical device. (3) A strange apparatus is set in front of the 'main' door, which should still be accessible. The apparatus will be used in the 'transformation' scene and is constructed from tubes, pipes and spheres ... see Appendix A. All this is masked by a screen with signs ... "Do Not Disturb", "Genius At Work", "Private", "Do Not Touch", "Danger", "Keep Out!", "Hands Off", "This Means You". (4) The 'kitchen' door is masked by a painted shelves of odd-looking inventions, bottles of chemicals and books.
There is a large, translucent screen D.C. which will be illuminated from behind for the 'shadow' operation. The bottom portion of the screen should be blacked-out to the height of the 'operating table' to conceal the props. Behind the screen: two pairs of boxing gloves, a long tube of material (stuffed), a pair of garden shears, a bunch of flowers, a wellington boot, a prop hand, a bugle, a telephone receiver & cord, a birthday cake, and a prop head.
There is a table beside the screen and on it: a carving knife & steel, a large prop mallet, a pair of socks, an electric drill, a saw, a washing-up bowl, a bottle of "Fairy Liquid", a spanner, bolts and an L.P. record.
The tabs open. MISS NELLY is behind the screen, dressed as a nurse. Off-stage, FRANKIE is quickly replaced on the trolley by a person of similar stature. Enter CRACKPOT R.)

Crackpot Nurse! Nurse!

Miss Nelly *(emerging from behind screen)* Yes, doctor?

Crackpot Is everything ready for the operation?

Miss Nelly Yes, doctor! *(she picks up the carving knife and sharpens it on the steel)*

Crackpot Excellent! *(calling off-right)* Wheel in the patient!
(Enter LUDWIG and HEIDI with the trolley, followed by KODAK)

Miss Nelly *(to audience)* This bit's going to be really gory so those of you with weak stomachs had better leave now.

Ludwig Where do you want him, Professor?

Crackpot Behind the screen. *(indicating audience)* We don't want our friends to faint. *(takes surgical mask from his pocket and puts it on)*
(LUDWIG and HEIDI wheel the trolley behind the screen)

Miss Nelly Why are you putting on that mask?

Crackpot So nobody can identify me if things go wrong! *(LUDWIG and HEIDI return)* Wunderbar! *(laughs insanely)* This will be my greatest experiment yet ... the creation of life! Lights!
(A bright light floods the screen from behind and the main lights dim. LUDWIG, HEIDI and KODAK sit at the side of the stage and watch)
(The following 'shadow operation' should be fast-paced. All movements should be exaggerated and care should be taken to display the props clearly in silhouette)

Crackpot First I must examine the patient. *(removes the sheet covering the victim, who groans and sits up)*

Miss Nelly The patient's waking up, Professor!

Crackpot Quickly ... administer the anaesthetic!

(MISS NELLY picks up the mallet, steps behind the screen and whacks the patient over the head - a drum-thud. The patient drops his head back and immediately raises his legs ... "boing" sound-effect. CRACKPOT grabs the legs and forces them down. The torso rises again)

Crackpot Quickly, nurse ... we need more anaesthetic!

Miss Nelly Yes, doctor! *(she fetches the pair of socks)*

Crackpot The strongest you've got!

Miss Nelly *(sniffing socks)* Phew! These would knock out a horse! *(she returns behind the screen and dangles them in the patient's face. A groan and the torso sinks back. She tosses the socks over the screen)*

Crackpot Good, good ... we are now ready to begin. Knife!

Miss Nelly *(fetching the knife)* Knife!

(CRACKPOT holds it up and plunges it into the patient, making an incision from top to bottom. Sound of a zip being opened. He drops the knife)

Crackpot Drill!

Miss Nelly *(passing him the electric drill)* Drill!

(He drills the head ... sound of dentist's [illegible] He drills the stomach ... sound of pnuematic drill. He drops the drill and plunges his hands into the stomach, pulling out a length of the tube)

Crackpot Grab this end! *(hands end to MISS NELLY)*

Together *(singing)* "Yo - oh - heave ho!
Yo - oh - heave ho!"

(They pull out huge lengths of tube. MISS NELLY emerges from behind screen tugging hard. The other end is held by the patient and appears to be stuck. CRACKPOT lifts the garden shears and 'cuts' the tube. MISS NELLY falls on her bottom - a drum thud)

Miss Nelly Watch what you're doing!

(She gets up and returns behind the screen. PROFESSOR CRACKPOT continues delving. "Plopping" noises as each of the following items are extracted)

Crackpot Where is it? I can't find it! *(holds up a bunch of flowers)* No that's not it. *(tosses the flowers over the screen)* Ah-ha! *(holds up a wellington-boot)* I've been looking for this for ages! *(throws it over the screen)* Nurse!

Miss Nelly Yes, doctor?

Crackpot I need your help ... have you got a free hand?

Miss Nelly *(holding up a prop hand)* Yes, doctor ... here you are!

Crackpot *(takes hand)* Thank you! *(tosses it over the screen)*

(They continue to search the patient. MISS NELLY pulls out a bugle and plays reveille ... CRACKPOT salutes. The bugle is tossed over the screen. A telephone rings. CRACKPOT plunges into the body and emerges with a receiver. The ringing stops)

Crackpot *(holding receiver to ear)* Hello? Yes? It's for you.

Miss Nelly *(taking receiver)* Hello? You don't say. You don't say! You don't say!! *(returns receiver)*

Crackpot Who was that?

Miss Nelly He didn't say!

Crackpot *(delving into body)* Eureka! I've found it! *(holds up prop cake)*

Together *(singing)* "Happy Birthday to you,
Happy Birthday to you,
Happy Birthday dear Frankenstein,
Happy Birthday to you"!

Miss Nelly Blow out the candles and make a wish!

(The patient sits up and blows. MISS NELLY gets the prop mallet and thumps him on the head ... the patient collapses. The cake is dropped)

Crackpot Enough of this!

Miss Nelly Enough of this!

Crackpot Off with his head!

Miss Nelly Off with his head!

Crackpot Saw!

Miss Nelly *(taking saw from table)* Saw! *(hands it to him)*

Crackpot Stand back!

Miss Nelly *(stepping into view)* Standing back, sir!

(CRACKPOT saws the head off ... sound of sawing. A drum-roll. He drops the saw and unscrews the head. A squeaking noise followed by a loud "pop" as the head comes off. MISS NELLY shrieks)

Crackpot *(throwing head)* Catch! *(she catches it)* Careful now ... don't lose your head!

Miss Nelly You're off your head! Catch! *(throws head back)*

Crackpot *(catching head)* Washing-up bowl!

Miss Nelly *(getting bowl)* Washing-up bowl!

Crackpot *(putting head into bowl)* "Fairy Liquid!"

Miss Nelly *(getting bottle)* "Fairy Liquid!" What are you doing?

Crackpot *(scrubbing at head)* Brain-washing!

Miss Nelly Isn't that a bit dangerous? A person can't live for long without a brain!

Crackpot You seem to be doing alright!

Miss Nelly Cheek!

Crackpot Almost finished! *(dropping bowl and fitting head back on body)* Now to put him back together again! Spanner!

Miss Nelly *(gets spanner and hands it to him)* Spanner!

Crackpot Bolts!

Miss Nelly *(gets bolts and hands them to him)* Bolts! *(he bolts on the head ... metallic squeaks)*

Crackpot Max Bygraves record!

Miss Nelly *(handing him L.P.)* Max Bygraves record!

(He places the record on the body and lifts the patient's arm up with the finger resting on the record like a stylus ... a few lines of a Max Bygrave's song is heard. He knocks the hand away ... sound of record being scratched)

Crackpot Lights!

(The flood light is switched off and the stage lights return. CRACKPOT and MISS NELLY push the screen aside. The body is now covered by the sheet. LUDWIG and HEIDI stand)

Heidi Was the operation successful, Professor?

Crackpot Wunderbar! Only one thing is missing!

Ludwig What's that?

Crackpot *(dramatically)* Donner und Blitzen! Thunder and lightning!

Miss Nelly "Electricity" to you. *(The lights flicker. KODAK looks skywards)*

Crackpot Ah-ha ... just in time! Eins, zwei, drei, fünf, sechs.

Ludwig *(over, to MISS NELLY)* What's he doing?

Miss Nelly Seeing how near the storm is. *(A rumble of thunder. KODAK cowers)*

Crackpot Six miles away! *(to LUDWIG)* Quick, Prince Nitwit, I shall need your help. We must wire him up before the storm reaches it's height! *(the wheel the trolley to the 'transformation apparatus' behind the decorated screen, thus enabling FRANKIE to replace the patient without being seen)*

Heidi I'll come too.

Miss Nelly No. You stay here and keep count. *(joins the others)*

(Occasional 'metallic' noices from behind the screen throughout the follwing)

Heidi *(to audience)* Oh dear. I hate storms, don't you? Especially in the middle of the night. They always give me a horrible, creepy feeling as if something terrible's going to happen any minute. *(the lights flicker)* More lightning. Help me keep count.

(As they count, GRANULA and DRACULA enter. They are thinly disguised as cleaning ladies: nylon overalls and wigs in curlers. They mop their way towards HEIDI)

Heidi One, two, three, four, five. *(a rumble of thunder. KODAK hides between her legs)* Five miles, Professor.

Crackpot *(shouting)* Good! *(to assistants)* Hurry, hurry.

Heidi *(patting KODAK)* It's alright, boy.

Granula Mind your feet! *(KODAK sniffs suspiciously)*

Heidi Sorry. Who are you?

Granula Emergency cleaners!

Dracula At your service!

Together If you're tired of scrubbing till you drop
Pick up that phone ... dial "Rent-A-Mop".

(They turn round. The overalls have a "Rent-A-Mop" logo on the back)

Heidi But we don't need any cleaners.

Granula Of course you do. Look at the state of this place.

Heidi Yes. It is a bit of a mess. *(the lights flicker)* Excuse me. *(DRACULA and GRANULA move away. KODAK follows suspiciously)* One, two, three, four. *(a rumble of thunder. KODAK hastily returns to HEIDI)* Four miles, Professor.

Crackpot How far? *(HEIDI moves to screen. KODAK follows)*

Heidi Four miles. *(looks behind screen)* Oh my goodness!

Granula *(to audience)* Hello, my dearios! *(lifting her wig and cackling)* You didn't recognise us, did you? *(puts wig back)*

Dracula I feel daft.

Granula Stop moaning. Do you want to catch Heidi, or not?

Dracula Yes. Let me at her! *(Lunges torward HEIDI. KODAK moves D.S., hackles up)*

Granula *(restraining him)* Not yet. We've got to put that pesky pooch out of action first. Now, where are they?

(They search among the props. The lights flicker and HEIDI returns)

Heidi Here we go again. *(flickering stops)* One, two, three. *(a rumble of thunder)* It's getting closer. *(calling)* Three miles Professor.

Crackpot Ja. Ja. *(metallic noises)* Eureka!

Heidi *(returning to screen)* Have you finished?

Crackpot Almost.

Dracula *(holding up pair of socks)* Eureka!

Granula Have you found them?

Crackpot Wunderbar!

Granula *(taking socks)* Wunderbar! *(sniffs them, pulls a face and holds them at arm's length)* Pooh! Just what the doctor ordered ... nice and ripe and pongy! *(HEIDI returns)* Quick, here she comes. *(holds socks behind back)* Act nonchalent. *(they lean on their mops and hum)*

Heidi Haven't you finished yet?

Granula Give us a chance.

Dracula *(holding up prop hand)* I've only got three hands you know!

Heidi Your faces look very familiar. Haven't we met somewhere before?

Granula Of course not. My name's Helga. And this is Brunhilde. *(DRACULA curtsies)*

Heidi How do you do. My name's Heidi.

Both Heidi hi!

(MISS NELLY, CRACKPOT and LUDWIG pop their heads round the corners to the screen)

Together Ho di ho! *(disappear again)*

Heidi This is Kodak. Say hello to the nice ladies, Kodak. *(KODAK growls)*

Dracula *(backing behind GRANULA)* Nice doggy, nice doggy.

Heidi I'm sorry. I don't know what's got into him.

Granula Here boy. Come on. I've got something for you.

Heidi What is it? A biscuit?

Granula No. Guess again.

Heidi A bone?

Granula No. *(producing socks)* These!

Dracula *(removing wig)* Sock it to him, Granny.

Heidi It's you!

Granula It's us.

Heidi *(releasing KODAK)* Get them, boy! *(KODAK barks and stalks them)*

Granula Yes, come and get them, flea-brain. *(She dangles the socks in KODAK's face. He swoons, legs in the air. DRACULA grabs HEIDI)*

Heidi Help! Help!
(MISS NELLY, CRACKPOT and LUDWIG come from behind the screen. DRACULA drags HEIDI to the side of the stage)

Ludwig Heidi!

Heidi Save me!

Ludwig Stop them!

Crackpot *(restraining him)* Look out ... she's got a pair of socks.

Granula Yes. And I'm not afraid to use them!

Crackpot Send for reinforcements!

Miss Nelly Good idea. *(shouting)* Agnes! Ethel! This way girls!
(Loud cheering. Enter GIRLS from stairs, armed with hockey sticks, followed by BUCKLES and any remaining members of the CHORUS. The GIRLS surround GRANULA)

Granula *(threatening with socks)* Stand back!

Miss Nelly Get her, girls!
(AGNES steps quickly behind GRANULA. A ripping noise. She reappears with a pair of green bloomers decorated with bats)

Agnes She won't get far without these! *(the girls cheer and wave their sticks)*

Granula *(patting her skirt in disbelief)* You grubby little minx ... give them back! *(She waves the socks into front of AGNES, who faints. The other girls charge. GRANULA spins around waving the socks and they all faint. The other principals step forward)* Come on then, who's next? *(They step back)* Ha ha ha! Cowardy, cowardy custards! *(she crosses to DRACULA)* Away with her!
(Exit DRACULA and GRANULA with HEIDI. The GIRLS and KODAK revive)

Ludwig *(moving L.)* Come back, Heidi!

Buckles *(restraining him)* It's no use, your highness! They're stronger than all of us put together!

Ludwig But we've got to do something to save her!

Crackpot I've got it. *(snaps fingers)*

Ludwig Oh, you have an idea!

Crackpot No ... I've just learnt to snap my fingers. *(the lights flicker)* Wait. One. Two. *(thunder)* Only two miles. *(to MISS NELLY)* Quick, nurse. There's only one person in the whole world who can save Heidi now. *(they move either side of the screen)*

Buckles Who's that?

Crackpot My new creation ... Frankenstein!
(They trolley is revealed. FRANKIE's body is covered and surrounded by a tangle of wires)

Girls Frankenstein?

Crackpot Ja. This is my Marvellous Monster Making Machine. With it, I Professor Crackpot, will create life out of death! *(laughs maniacally and fiddles with the apparatus)* The lighting strikes here ... "crrrash"! Comes down here ... "bzzzzt". Then I pull this lever and hey presto! *(the lights flicker)*

Miss Nelly Stand back everybody ... the lightning is about to strike.

(Thunder. CRACKPOT pulls a lever. Simultaneous thunder and lightning. A puff of smoke. Flashing lights)

Crackpot *(heavenwards)* More electricity. More. Bring Frankie back to life! Ha ha. *(returns lever)* That should do it. *(to MISS NELLY)* Unplug the patient.

Miss Nelly Yes, Professor. *(She removes the wiring. CRACKPOT feels for a pulse)*

Ludwig Has it worked?

Crackpot *(shaking head)* I can't feel a pulse. *(moves away from trolley)*

Miss Nelly We did our best for him.

Girls Poor Frankie!

Ludwig Now there's nobody to rescue Heidi! *(BRIDGET comforts him)*

(FRANKIE raises an arm under the sheet)

Crackpot Wait! He moved!

Miss Nelly He's alive!

(FRANKIE sits up, still covered with the sheet. ALL cheer. CRACKPOT pulls the sheet off. Everyone gasps. FRANKIE's skin is now green, there are stitch-marks on his forehead and he has a bolt through the neck. He is sucking his thumb)

Crackpot Ah! Isn't he cute?

Miss Nelly I don't think he recognises you.

Frankie Daddy! *(cuddles CRACKPOT)*

Crackpot *(painfully)* Arrgh. Let go. There's a good boy. *(CRACKPOT and MISS NELLY help him off the trolley)*

Frankie Ooo, what happened? I feel ever so funny.

Crackpot You're still a bit woozy.

Miss Nelly Easy does it.

Frankie *(pointing at audience)* What are all these people doing here?

Miss Nelly You remember them. They're all your friends.

Frankie Oh yes. *(waving)* Hello boys and girls.

Audience Hello, Frankie.

Frankie *(noticing hand)* Arrgh! My hand's turned green. So's the other one.

Crackpot Nothing to worry about!

Frankie *(feeling face)* What have you done to me? *(touching bolts)* What's this?

Miss Nelly *(pulling his hands away)* Don't touch!

Frankie Why not?

Miss Nelly You're head will fall off! *(giving him a mirror)* See what I mean?

Frankie Ugh! I'm a big, ugly monster.

Crackpot Nonsense. You look like a million dollars.

Frankie Yes, all green a wrinkled! *(examines face in mirror)* I'm horrific!

Miss Nelly You're terrific! *(to audience)* Isn't he?

All Yes.

Frankie If you say so. *(KODAK whines and paws FRANKIE)*

Frankie What's wrong boy?

Miss Nelly He's trying to tell you the bad news.

Crackpot It's Heidi.

Ludwig She's been kidnapped.

Miss Nelly There's been a Heidi hijack!
All Ho-di-ho!
Ludwig Now, Frankenstein, it's up to you
To get poor Heidi back
Crackpot To put an end to Granula
And pulverise Count Drac. !
Frankie I'll go to where the vampire's are
And batter down the doors
And Granula will not get far!
Agnes Well, not without her drawers! *(waves bloomers)*
Bridget We'll come along and lend a hand!
Ethel We'll biff and bash and swot 'em!
Miss Nelly I'll put Count Drac. across my knee
And then ... I'll smack his bottom!
Ludwig Knickers!

SONG G
Principals & Chorus

Crackpot Welcome now my new creation:
A masterpiece of transplantation!
Frankie Are you sure I look fine?
Crackpot Would I feed you a line?
Take it from me: everybody loves Frankie!
Frankie Once I was just pale and scrawny
But now I've turned out green and brawny!
And who gives a heck
About bolts through the neck?
Now I'm something to see!
All Everybody loves Frankie!
Someone who was weak and sappy
Has the power to make our ending happy.
Now you're Frankenstein
You're the toast of the Rhine.
Believe what you see: everybody loves Frankie!
From head to toe, a man-made wonder!
You're complete: you're super-spectacular!
Made to pull the rug from under-neath the feet
Of Granny and Dracula!
So stamp your feet and give a hand to
The hero of our monster panto.
He's a fabulous star
And he's sure to go far!
The whole world agrees: Everybody loves Frankie!

End of Act One

Act Two
Scene 1
Dracula's Castle

(This scene uses the same basic set as Act One - see Appendix A for details.
The overall appearance of the set should be of neglected grandeur and ruined opulence, for example ... a mouldering tapestry, shredded flags, a coat of arms (bat sinister and lightning dexter), a vile portrait of Dracula as a baby, monstrous 'animal' heads, cobwebs, litter, graffiti.
There is a stained-glass window, a staircase and two exits U.S. with signs above them: "The Dungeons" and "The Ballroom". There are two further exits D.L. and D.R.
A large, ornate throne is set on a rostra U.S. This has a hinged seat and a false back, allowing access from behind. A pair of lady's slippers and an alarm clock lie on the floor beside it.
Stage-right is a fully draped dining-table and three chairs. The table butts into the wings, allowing access underneath. There is a hole in the centre hidden by a large, silver food-cover. On the table are the festering left-overs of a bygone feast, two custard pies, a prop club, a vase of dead flowers, a tray of condiments and a wax-encrusted candelabra.
A large, 'coffin-shaped' grandfather clock stands L., facing the auditorium. It has a false back to allow access from the wings. The entire front of the clock is a 'door' and the clock face can open independently. There is a hole, at waist level, large enough for a hand.
Spooky sound effects. The stage is filled with smoke and is very dark: the only light comes through the stained glass window. Intro music. Enter the CHORUS and/or DANCERS, as ghosts. A short ballet sequence (optional).
The music continues. Enter FRANKIE D.L. holding a prop club. The GHOSTS hide around the stage)

Frankie *(to audience)* Hello everybody. *(the audience responds)* So this is Dracula's Castle! It's awfully spooky, isn't it? But don't you worry. *(waving club)* I've got my monster-masher with me. And that's not all ... I've also got my brave team of ghost-busters! *(calling off)* Come one, everybody! *(sings)*

SONG H
Ensemble

(Enter MISS NELLY, BUCKLES, LUDWIG, KODAK and the principal SCHOOLGIRLS. They search the stage, are scared by the GHOSTS who are in turn clobbered by FRANKIE and chased off. The song ends and the last GHOST exits. ALL cheer)

Frankie That's got rid of the spooks.
Miss Nelly Now all we have to do is find Heidi.
Frankie *(to audience)* Have any of you seen her?
Audience No.
Frankie That's a pity.
Ludwig We must rescue her before it's too late. *(sits miserably on a chair)*
Agnes Yes. Look at the time. *(points at grandfather clock)* It'll be dark soon.
Ethel *(fearfully)* And then the vampires will wake up.
Frankie *(brandishing club)* Don't worry about them ... I'll pulverise them to pieces.
Mabel You'll have to find them first!

Constance Vampires are very sneaky. They could be hiding anywhere.

Frankie Let's split up and scour the castle.

Miss Nelly Yes, it could do with a good clean.

Frankie You all look for Heidi. Leave Dracula and Granula to me. If you see anything suspicious, just shout "Frankie" and I'll come running. *(to audience)*
I'll search the castle high and low
And track down those two grots
And when I get my hands on them
I'll tie their fangs in knots! *(exits D.R.)*

Buckles *(to MISS NELLY)* We'll check the ballroom.

Miss Nelly "The Ballroom"? How posh!

Buckles *(bowing)* Would you care to dance, cheri?

Miss Nelly *(curtseying)* Enchante, m'sieur. *(They waltz into the Ballroom)*

Ludwig *(tearfully)* Poor Heidi! Will I ever see her again?

Bridget Forget her! She's probably been vamped by now!

Ludwig Vamped? *(he sobs and KODAK howls)*

Bridget Cheer up, Luddy darling ... you've got me now! *(LUDWIG stops crying, takes one look at her and sobs even louder)* Charming!

Agnes Don't worry, your highness. We'll find her even if we have to search the castle from top to bot... *(LUDWIG stands up with a glazed expression and opens his mouth)*

Ludwig Kniii ...

Mabel *(clapping a hand over AGNES's mouth)* Don't say it!

Ludwig *(to AGNES, recovering)* You're right. I mustn't give up hope. *(to KODAK)* Come on, boy. Maybe Heidi's imprisoned in the dungeons. *(KODAK follows)*

Bridget Wait for me.

Ludwig No. You stay here and keep look out.

Bridget Alright. On one condition: give me a kiss first.

Ludwig Oh, very well. Shut your mouth and close your eyes. *(she closes her eyes and purses her lips)* And prepare yourself for a big surprise. *(he whispers in KODAK's ear)*

Bridget What's keeping you?

Ludwig Nothing. Are you ready for your kiss?

Bridget Ready. *(She purses her lips again. KODAK jumps up and licks her. She splutters. Exit LUDWIG and KODAK to the Dungeons. She wipes her face and the other girls fall about laughing)* Pooh, what a sloppy kisser! *(to others)* Did you see that? He kissed me! I'm never going to wash my face again! *(sings)* "Some day my prince will come ... " *(snatches a flower from the vase on the table and plucks petals)* He loves me. He loves me not. *(Etc. She moves to the grandfather clock and stands with her back to it)*

Agnes Get her!

Ethel Makes you sick!

Mabel *(bellowing)* Coo-ee! Bloggsy!

Constance She's away with the fairies. *(they move away)*

Agnes Somebody pinch her, please!

(Drumroll. A hand appear through the hole in the clock and takes aim)

Bridget *(plucking last petal)* He loves me! Hooray! *(The hand pinches her bottom and disappears. Cymbal)* Ouch! Who did that?

Agnes Did what?

Bridget Somebody pinched me!

Ethel *(looking around)* Where?

Bridget On the ... *(quick glance towards the Dungeons)* b.o.t.t.o.m.

Ethel No. Who pinched you?

Mabel There's nobody here but us and them. *(points at audience)*

Constance *(to audience)* Did you see something? *(audience responds)*

Ethel What was it?

Mabel A hand?

Agnes Where was it? What? The clock?

Audience Yes.

Ethel They're daft. *(moving to clock)* All clocks have hands. *(pointing at clockface)* Anyone can see that!

Mabel You must have been imagining things!

Bridget *(encouraging audience)* Oh no we weren't!

Others Oh yes you were!

(Continue. ETHEL leans forward, hands on hips and backside protruding. The hand reappears, takes aim and pinches her)

Ethel Arrgh! He got me!

Agnes Who got you?

Ethel The phantom botty-pincher, that's who!

Constance *(to audience)* Did you see anybody that time?

Agnes Well where are they? What **inside** the clock?

Bridget Told you so.

Agnes Lets take a look. *(all go to clock)* I'll open it up and you bash them! *(the others raise their hockey sticks)* Ready?

Others Ready! *(AGNES opens the clock. It is empty. She closes clock again)*

Ethel There's nobody there.

Agnes *(to audience)* You rotten fibbers. *(rolling up sleeves)* I'm going to give you a piece of my mind!

Mabel You'd better not ... there wouldn't be much left! *(AGNES hits her)*

(Sound of an approaching electric vehicle)

Bridget Shshsh! I can hear something.

(Sound of bottles rattling and an echoing, tuneless whistle)

Ethel What is it?

Agnes Dunno. *(pointing off)* It's coming from over there!

(A spectral MILKMAN enters D.L. with a crate. He deposits two milk bottles, one containing red liquid and the other white, in front of the throne. The GIRLS form a terrified huddle)

Mabel Wh-wh-who's th-that?

Constance Search m-m-me!

All Frankie! Frankie!

Constance He can't hear us. *(to audience)* Give us a hand to shout for Frankie.

All Frankie!

(Enter FRANKIE D.R. as the MILKMAN exits D.L.)

Frankie What is it?

Girls A spook!

Frankie Where? There's nothing here.

Agnes That's strange. It was here a second ago.

Frankie You're up to your pranks again! *(pointing D.R.)* There's no sign of vampires that way ... I'll try upstairs. *(goes upstairs)*

Constance *(to audience)* There was a spook, wasn't there?

Audience Yes. *(Sound of bicycle bell ringing)*

Ethel Listen!

Bridget What?

Ethel I can hear bells.

(Enter a ghoulish NEWSBOY D.L. on a bicycle. The delivery bag slung over his shoulder says "Transylvanian Times". The GIRLS clutch each other again. The NEWSBOY stops in front of the grandfather clock and thrusts a newspaper into the hole)

Constance *(to audience)* Quick! Shout for Frankie.

All Frankie!

(FRANKIE enters from upstairs as the NEWSBOY exits D.R.)

Frankie Now what's wrong?

Girls A spook!

Frankie Where? You rotten tricksters! I've got a good mind to smack your bot ... *(quick glance towards Dungeons)* ... posteriors! *(returns to stairs)*

Constance *(to audience)* But we did see a spook, didn't we?

Audience Yes!

Frankie *(to audience)* You're as bad as them! *(exits upstairs)*

Agnes *(calling after him)* We can prove it. *(pointing at newspaper)* Look at this.

Ethel He's gone.

Agnes There's something fishy going on here and I'm going to get to the bot ... find the answer. *(reaches for newspaper)*

Constance Don't touch it!

(AGNES touches the newspaper and the clock immediately starts striking the prelude to the hour. The light through the stained-glass window starts to fade)

Constance *(pulling her back)* Now look what you've done. You've made it go off.

(Spotlight on the clockface: the hands move round)

Ethel Look! The hands are moving.

Mabel And it's getting dark.

Bridget *(nervously)* You know what that means, don't you?

All It's vampire time!

Ethel *(moving away)* Let's get out of here!

Agnes Send for re-inforcements!

(They exit D.L. The clock continues striking and an alarm clock rings. The spotlight focuses on the throne. Creaking noises. The seat rises. A gnarled hand emerges, holding a mallet and whacks the alarm clock. Sound of springs breaking and the bell stops. GRANULA stands up, yawning and stretching. Her hair is in curlers and she wears a ghastly nightdress. She steps out of the throne and notices the audience)

Granula Curses! What are you lot doing here? This is private property. Buzz off! *(she steps into the slippers, picks up the 'milk' bottles, drags her feet across to the dining table and puts the bottles down)* Nosey parkers! Always interfering where they're not wanted. *(to audience)* Are you still here? Well, it doesn't matter. You wouldn't dare tell anyone about my secret hideout, would you?

Audience Yes!

Granula You'd better not! Us vampires are so sneaky! I bet you can't guess where Dracula's hiding, can you? I'll give you a clue. *(knocking on clock)* Knock knock!

(DRACULA is inside the clock. He opens the clock-face)

Dracula Who's there?

Granula Little old lady.

Dracula Little old lady who? *(pushing his head out)*

Granula I didn't know you could yodel! *(slams the clock-face on him)* Time to get up!

(GRANULA shuffles across to above the table as the clock opens. DRACULA is wearing a bed-cap and a dressing gown. He rubs his nose painfully, steps out of the clock, picks up the newspaper and crosses to GRANULA)

Granula Breakfast's ready.

Dracula Goody, goody gumboils. I'm famished.

Granula Sit yourself down and I'll pour you a nice, thick glass of blood. *(holds up bottles)*

Dracula Is it fresh? *(sits and opens newspaper)*

Granula Of course it's fresh ... the bloodman's just delivered it. Red or white corpuscle?

Dracula Red.

Granula *(filling a glass)* Here you are. Hurry up and drink it before it clots.

Dracula *(raising glass)* Cheers. *(reads paper)*

Granula Bottoms up!

Ludwig *(distant voice)* Knickers!

Granula Who said that? *(DRACULA chortles)* What are you laughing at?

Dracula I'm just reading my favourite column.

Granula What's that ... the **horror**scope?

Dracula No. "Deaths".

Granula You mean, the "O-**bite**-uary"! *(gnashes gums)*

Dracula I say, that's odd. I can't find Heidi's name anywhere.

Granula Of course not. She isn't dead yet!

Dracula *(laying down paper)* Isn't dead?

Granula *(innocently)* She's been saved.

Dracula *(disappointed)* Saved?

Granula Yes. *(gleefully)* Saved for breakfast! *(she lifts the food-cover. HEIDI's head is underneath)*

Heidi You fiends!

Dracula "Yummy, yummy", says my tummy. *(ties serviette round neck)*

Heidi Let me out of here!

Granula Relax, sweetheart, you're not going anywhere. *(lifting tray of condiments)* So why don't you join us for breakfast?

Heidi What are you having?

Dracula & Granula You! *(together)*

Heidi Keep away from me!

Granula *(to DRACULA)* A sprinkling of pepper?

Dracula It'll make her taste better.

Granula Salt and sauce?

Dracula But of course!

Heidi Ugh! Stop it!

Granula A dollop of cream?

Dracula Sounds like a dream. *(GRANULA sprays foam over HEIDI)*

Heidi Get off me! *(DRACULA whisks a finger across her head)*

Dracula Mmmm! Positively droolsome. *(lunges forward)*

Granula Wait! You haven't said grace yet.

Dracula Oh yes. For what I am about to received my the Lord make me truly **fang**-ful. *(bares fangs and leans over HEIDI)*

Heidi Go ahead. I'll be brave.

Dracula Drat! She's not screaming. It's no fun unless they scream.

Granula Aren't you frightened?

Heidi No. My friends will be here any minute ... they'll save me! *(to audience)* Won't they?

Audience Yes!

Granula Rubbish!

Heidi Help! Help! *(to audience)* Quick everybody ... whistle for Kodak!
(The audience whistles. GRANULA slams the cover over HEIDI. Barking off-stage)

Granula Rats! It's that curs-ed canine!

Dracula Let's get out of here!
(Enter KODAK from the Dungeons, barking ferociously. He chases them. DRACULA escapes into the clock, GRANULA into the throne, leaving the seat up)

Ludwig *(voice off)* Kodak! Kodak! Here, boy! *(Enter LUDWIG from the Dungeons. KODAK sniffs around the stage)* There you are! That's strange. There's nobody here. I could have sworn I heard Heidi cry.

Dracula *(opening clock face)* Ho di ho! *(disappears)*

Ludwig Who said that? *(KODAK puts his paws up on the table and barks)* What is it, boy? Do you want some din-dins? *(KODAK shakes his head. To audience)* Do you know what he wants? What? Heidi! Where is she? *(going left)* Is she over here?

Audience No! *(KODAK shakes his head)*

Ludwig Is she upstairs?

Audience No! *(KODAK shakes his head)*

Ludwig *(moving to table)* Is she over here?

Audience Yes! *(KODAK nods)*

Ludwig Where abouts? *(KODAK barks)* I see ... she's under here. Well, let's take a look then!

(He lifts the lid. Underneath is a skeleton's head ... we hear amplified laughter. He looks horrified for a few seconds and then hastily replace the lid)

Ludwig Help me call for Frankie

All Frankie! *(Enter FRANKIE from upstairs. KODAK sniffs around the stage)*

Frankie What's wrong?

Ludwig It's a sk-sk-sk-sk ...

Frankie A "sk-sk"?

Ludwig Skeleton! Under there! It was awful!

Frankie *(taking hold of cover)* I'm not frightened of skeletons ... they're just a pile of bones with the person scraped off! *(lifts cover)* Arrgh! *(Margaret Thatcher's head, or some current political figure, is underneath (a mask))* It's Maggie! Keep away! Get back!

Ludwig Maybe if you ask her nicely, she'll go away ... reason with her. *(moves to the throne)*

Frankie She never listens to reason. *(replaces cover)* That's better.

Ludwig What a fright. I'd better sit down for a minute. *(sits and falls inside with his legs protruding)* Arrgh! Help!

Frankie *(grabbing his legs)* Hang on. I've got you. *(hauls him out)*

Ludwig What happened?

Frankie *(peering inside)* It looks like some kind of secret passage. Or a well.

Ludwig Well, well!

Frankie *(picking up alarm clock)* I wonder how deep it is.

Ludwig What are you doing?

Frankie Killing time.

(He drops the clock. Swannee whistle. They watch it descend. A distant cra

Granula *(echoing voice off)* Ow! Who did that?

Ludwig There's somebody down there. Maybe it's Heidi. *(shouting into throne)* Heidi hi!

Granula *(off)* Ho-di-ho!

Ludwig It is Heidi. *(climbs in)* Don't worry, my darling, I'll save you. *(disappears)*

Frankie It didn't sound like Heidi. *(to audience)* Is she down there? No? Who is it then? Granula! Wait till I get my hands on her ... *(waving club)* I'll granulate her!

(He climbs inside and disappears. KODAK looks inside the throne, whines and wags his tail. As FRANKIE disappears GRANULA appears at the back of the auditorium carrying a large 'butterfly' net. KODAK looks into the throne, whines and wags his tail)

Granula *(to audience, moving towards stage)* Surprise, suprise. You didn't expect to see me here, did you? Nincompoops! This castle's full of secret passages and we know everyone of them! *(loud whisper)* Pssst! Dracula!

(She climbs onto the stage. The clock-face opens and DRACULA looks out)

Dracula Ja?

Granula It's time we got rid of that pesky-pooch. Are you ready?

Dracula Yes, Granny.

(DRACULA pushes a fishing rod, with a bone dangling from the end, through the hole)

Granula Excellent. Let's go fishing! *(to audience)* Dog-fishing! *(she hides D.S. of the table)*

Dracula *(shouting)* Here doggy, doggy. Here's a nice bone for you!

(KODAK turns. DRACULA waves the bone around. KODAK spots it and pads across, sniffing. DRACULA tantalises him as GRANULA sneaks up behind. She nets KODAK. A struggle. DRACULA withdraws the fishing rod)

Granula Gotcha! Keep still, you stupid mutt. You can't escape.

Dracula That'll teach you!

Granula *(to audience)* You can whistle all you like now. It won't do any good.

Dracula There's nobody in the whole wide world strong enough to defeat us now!

(Waltz music)

Granula Shsh! Quiet! There's someone coming. Get out of sight. We'll pick the rest of them off one by one!

(She drags KODAK off to the Dungeons and DRACULA slams the clock-face. MISS NELLY and BUCKLES waltz on from the Ballroom. They stop D.C.)

Miss Nelly *(to audience)* The ballroom was completely empty.

Buckles Yes. There was nowhere for Heidi to hide.

Dracula *(opening clock-face)* Ho-di-ho!

Miss Nelly What was that?

Buckles It must have been the speaking clock.

Miss Nelly That's alright then. How about another dance?

Buckles Why not!

(Music. They waltz around the stage. DRACULA enters from the clock and taps BUCKLES on the shoulder. He steps back to let DRACULA dance with MISS NELLY before doing a 'double-take'. He screams and runs into the auditorium. MISS NELLY and DRACULA continue dancing for a few moments. The music stops)

Miss Nelly Wunderbar, Buckles! *(simpering)* You're so nimble on your toes! *(holding out her cheek)* You may kiss me on the cheek, if you like! *(DRACULA bares his fangs and goes for her neck. She knocks him back)* I said my cheek, not my neck! *(sees DRACULA for the first time)* Dracula! Arrgh! Mummy!

(A chase through the auditorium. The SCHOOLGIRLS, principals and chorus, sing the "School Anthem" offstage. DRACULA stops and listens. MISS NELLY and BUCKLES exit at back of auditorium. DRACULA returns to the stage and exits into the clock. The GIRLS march on. CONSTANCE is carrying a book,

AGNES has a giant stick of dynamite, MABEL a detonator box and ETHEL a coil of wire)

SONG I

The Schoolgirls

Agnes *(to audience)* We're back! The vampires don't stand a chance now, do they girls? *(The GIRLS cheer and jeer)*

Bridget *(to CONSTANCE)* Are you sure you know what you're doing?

Constance It's dead simple. It says so in this book.

Bridget *(reading cover)* "Home-made Bombs" by Dinah Mite.

Constance *(reading instructions)* "Uncoil wire."

Ethel *(doing so)* Uncoiling wire, sir! *(salutes)*

Constance "Take stick of explosive".

Agnes Explosive took, sir! *(salutes and bashes herself with stick)* Ouch!

Constance Careful! That's dynamite. Don't drop it, or the whole of *(local town)* will go up in a puff of smoke! "Attach wire to explosive."

Agnes Who's got the wire?

Ethel I have.

Agnes Catch!

(She tosses the dynamite to ETHEL. She misses and it drops to the ground. ALL shriek, cover their ears and cower. Nothing happens. ETHEL picks up the dynamite and attaches the wire)

Constance *(hitting AGNES)* Clumsy clot! "Fix other end of wire to detonator".

Mabel *(doing so)* Fixing detonator, sir! *(to audience)* This is the best way to catch vampires. Set a trap. Light the fuse. And *(shouting)* BANG! *(ALL jump)*

Bridget Shsh! Don't give the game away. Someone might be listening! *(As she speaks: DRACULA opens the clock-face and looks out; the food-cover is raised and GRANULA appears)* Walls have ears! *(DRACULA and GRANULA vanish as they turn to look. Sound of approaching footsteps)*

Mabel There's someone coming!

Agnes It must be Dracula! Action stations!

Ethel We'll blast him to smithereens! *(sets the dynamite D.L.)*

Bridget Hurry up ... he's getting closer!

Agnes Take cover! *(They crouch in front of the table. To CONSTANCE)* Now what?

Constance *(consulting book)* It says here, "Count 5 backwards, and shout "Bingo" at the top of your voice!"

Agnes Right! *(to audience)* You'll help us, won't you?

Audience Yes! *(MABEL and raises the plunger on the detonator box)*

Agnes Off we go then. Five, four ...

All ... three, two, one ... BINGO!

(The girls all cover their ears as MABEL depresses the plunger. A flash and an explosion. Enter CRACKPOT, clutching a paper bag, and MISS NELLY. Both are in charred, tattered clothing and stagger across the stage)

Agnes Got him! *(GIRLS cheer)*

Crackpot Where am I?

Constance Ooops!

Agnes What a waste of dynamite!

Miss Nelly You little horrors!

Crackpot What happened?

Miss Nelly *(guiding CRACKPOT to table)* You've had a nasty shock. Come on and sit yourself down and have a nice cup of tea. *(The food-cover rises and a hand appears holding a cup and saucer. She takes it)* Ta! There you are Professor. *('double take' - she grabs the food cover, lifts it and finds nothing)*

Agnes Let's get out of here! *(GIRLS make a run for the exits)*

Miss Nelly Come back! Attention! *(the GIRLS line up)* Repeat after me ... "I must not ..."

Girls I must not ...

Miss Nelly ... "blow up my teacher"!

Agnes But, Miss, we weren't trying to blow you up, we were ...

Miss Nelly Silence! Now, as a punishment, you clean this place from top to bot ... the other place.

Girls Awww, Miss!

Miss Nelly At once!

SONG J

The Schoolgirls

(Cleaning equipment is passed on from the wings. The GIRLS synchronise their actions as they sing: washing the floor, wringing out cloths, standing up, wiping brows, thumping down buckets, sweeping, etc. MISS NELLY stands attentively beside CRACKPOT. The song ends and the props are passed off-stage again. The GIRLS stand exhausted)

Miss Nelly That's better! Now say you're sorry to Professor Crackpot.

Girls We're sorry, Professor Crackpot.

Constance But Miss, we we're only trying to blow up Dracula!

Crackpot Blow on! Blow on!

Miss Nelly Yes dear, you blow on your tea if it's too hot.

Crackpot No, no ... you can't kill vampires with blowing up ... only with blowing on! *(holds up paper bag)* Eureka! Success at last!

Miss Nelly What is it?

Crackpot Vampire-vanquishers!

Miss Nelly Eh?

Crackpot *(taking a mint from the bag)* Perfect peppermints! Who want's one? *(CRACKPOT is swamped by the GIRLS)*

Miss Nelly *(pulling them off)* One at a time. Get back. Greedy little pigs. Gerroff! Attention! *(GIRLS stand at attention. CRACKPOT is sitting on the floor in a state of shock, still holding out the bag)* Where's your manners! Now say you're sorry to Professor Crackpot.

Girls Mnn mnn mnn!

Miss Nelly And don't speak with your mouths full. Now who wants to go and look for Dracula and give him the breath of death?

Girls *(waving arms)* Me! Me! Me! Me!

Miss Nelly Alright, Mimi ... you can go ... the rest of you stay here. *(all the GIRLS cheer and exit to the Dungeons, except BRIDGET)* Run along, Bridget.

Bridget But please, Miss ... I never got a peppermint, Miss.

Miss Nelly Well, hurry up!

(BRIDGET feels in the bag, still held in CRACKPOT's outstreached hand)

Bridget Rats!

Miss Nelly Now what's wrong?

Bridget There isn't any left, Miss.

Miss Nelly Let me see! Oh yes there is.

Bridget Where?

Miss Nelly There ... at the bottom.

(LUDWIG appears at back of the auditorium and walks to the stage)

Ludwig Knickers!

Crackpot *(coming to)* Oh dear, oh dear! How embarrassing.

Ludwig *(to audience)* This place is riddled with secret passages.

Crackpot Forgive me, your highness.

Ludwig What for? *(climbs onto stage)*

Crackpot I meant to snap you out it ages ago.

Ludwig Snap me out of what?

Crackpot Just take a look at this. *(Rips open lab-coat. MISS NELLY and BRIDGET recoil. He takes the hypno-gun)* It'll all be over with in seconds.

(LUDWIG looks confused. BRIDGET shields him)

Bridget Don't shoot him, Professor ... I love him.

Crackpot I'm not going to shoot him. I'm going to de-hypnotise him! *(To LUDWIG, using the gun. Electronic beeping noises)* Now listen carefully, Prince Ludwig ... I am going to count to three and snap my fingers and when I do you will wake up and forget all about this 'knicker' nonsense. Do you understand?

Ludwig *(in a trance)* I understand and will obey.

Crackpot Good. One. Two. Three. *(he attempts to snap his fingers and fails. He hands the hypno-gun to BRIDGET who examines it eagerly)* Hold this! Try again. *(he snaps the fingers of his 'gun' hand. LUDWIG awakes)* Now just to make sure ... *(shouting)* ... bottom!!

Ludwig What are you talking about?

Crackpot Good, good ... excellent!

Bridget *(taking LUDWIG's arm)* Hello, darling. Remember me?

Ludwig *(pushing her away)* Excuse me. I've got to find Heidi. *(exits to the Ballroom)* Heidi! Where are you, sweetheart?

Bridget *(stamping foot)* All he ever thinks about is that goody-two-shoes. He never even notices me. *(looks at gun, idea forming)* Professor, how does this hypno-gun work?

Crackpot Just point it and pull the trigger. *(holds hand out for it)*

Bridget Brilliant! *(runs after LUDWIG)* Ludwig! Yoo-hoo! I've got something to show you. *(exit to the Ballroom)*

Crackpot *(chasing after her)* Give me back my gun! Come back here ... *(exit)*

Miss Nelly Wait. Don't leave me alone here. They've gone. And I never even got a peppermint. *(to audience)* You'll stay and keep me company, won't you? Thanks. I don't know about you, but this place gives me the screaming hab-dabs. *(Sits on edge of the throne)* You know, wherever I go I keep getting this funny feeling that there's somebody just behind me, breathing down my neck! *(GRANULA appears from the throne and grabs her)*

Granula Gotcha!

Miss Nelly Arrgh! Frankie! Frankie! *(Enter FRANKIE D.R.)*

Frankie *("dalek" voice)* Exterminate! *(Whacks GRANULA. Swannee whistle, descending screech and thump)* Got her! *(looking into the throne)*

Miss Nelly Is she dead?

Granula *(distant voice)* I'll get you for this!

Frankie Nope.

Miss Nelly My hero! Oh, Frankie, you're so big and green and strong. You may collect your reward. *(opens arms and purses lips)*

Frankie What for?

Miss Nelly For saving a damsel in distress.

Frankie *(pointing at her dress)* But you're in 'dis' dress and you're no damsel. *(moves to the grandfather clock)*

Miss Nelly *(following)* Don't be rotten. Everyone says that my beauty is timeless.

Frankie Yes ... your face would stop a clock! *(He examines the front of the clock)*

Miss Nelly Huh! Your no prize-guy yourself. Have you found Heidi yet?

Frankie No. I've searched every room and been through been every secret passage and still no sign of her. *(He moves to the D.S. side of the clock. A hand emerges from the clock and feels around)*

Miss Nelly What about Dracula and Granula?

Frankie No. I can't find them either. But I've got a feeling that they're somewhere close by.

(The hand touches MISS NELLY's bottom)

Miss Nelly Oh! *(simpering)* Frankie! There's children present. Keep your hands to yourself.

Frankie I'm not doing anything.

Miss Nelly *(turning)* Someone's doing something. *(turns and sees hand)* Eek! Look. *(the hand disappears)*

Frankie What?

Miss Nelly A hand.

Frankie I thought there was something fishy about this clock. *(to audience)* Has someone been hiding in here?

Audience Yes.

Frankie Who was it?

Audience Dracula.

Miss Nelly Dracula! Eeek.

Frankie Good. I've been waiting for this. *(bashes on clock with club)* Come out of and fight like a man.

Miss Nelly But he's not a man.

Frankie You're right. *(bashing on clock)* Come out and fight like a monster. *(the hand emerges)* Quick. Grab a hold. *(MISS NELLY grabs the hand)* And don't let go till I've bashed him.

Miss Nelly Hurry up. He's too strong for me.

Frankie Here we go. One. Two. Three.

(He opens the clock. HEIDI is crouching on the other side. FRANKIE stops himself hitting her just in time)

Heidi Ouch. Let go!

Frankie Heidi!

Heidi *(backing into clock)* Keep away from me you horrible monster.

Frankie Don't you recognise me? It's me ... Frankie.

Heidi Frankie? Thank goodness. *(hugs him)*

Miss Nelly What were you doing in there?

Heidi Trying to get out. I've been wandering around in the dark for ages. I thought I'd never escape.

Miss Nelly Don't worry. You're safe now.

Frankie Nobody's safe with Dracula still at large. Not to mention Granula.

Miss Nelly *(clutching throat)* Granula!

Frankie I said not to mention Granula. *(hits her with club)* I've looked everywhere and still haven't caught them.

Heidi What are we going to do?

Frankie Search me!

Miss Nelly *(frisking him)* Alright!

Frankie Gerroff!

Heidi I've got it!

Miss Nelly Well don't give it to us!

Heidi There's only one thing to do.

Frankie What's that?

Heidi If *you* can't find Dracula ... wait for him to find *us*.

Frankie You what?

Heidi You've got to set your trap.

Miss Nelly And then what?

Heidi Shut your trap!

Miss Nelly Well, I only asked.

Heidi I'll be the bait. *(pushing FRANKIE into clock)* And you lie in wait.

Frankie Brilliant!

Miss Nelly It sounds awfully dangerous.

Heidi I'll be alright. Our friends will help. *(to audience)* Won't you?

Audience Yes.

Heidi When the vampires grab me, we'll whistle for Kodak and he'll corner them. And then we'll call for Frankie ...

Frankie *(brandishing club)* And I'll clobber them! *(closes clock)*

Heidi Yoo-hoo! Dracula! Come and get me!

Miss Nelly *(fearfully)* Not so loud. He'll hear you.
Heidi That's the idea. Yoo-hoo!
Ludwig *(off)* Yoo-hoo!
Miss Nelly Oh, he's coming. Quickly Heidi, hide!
(FRANKIE opens the clock-face as LUDWIG enters)
All Ho-di-ho! *(FRANKIE disappears)*
Heidi Ludwig!
Ludwig *(stopping)* Heidi!
Heidi *(opening arms)* Ludwig!
Ludwig *(opening arms)* Heidi! *(they run into to each others arms)*
Bridget *(voice off)* Ludwig!
Ludwig I've been worried sick about you.
Heidi I thought I'd never see you again. *(kisses her)*

SONG K
Ludwig & Heidi

(The song ends. Enter BRIDGET from the Ballroom)
Miss Nelly Ahh. Isn't that nice?
Heidi Safe at last.
Ludwig I'll take care of you.
Bridget *(to audience)* I'll take care of her!
Ludwig *(feeling in pocket)* I've got something for you.
Bridget I've got something for him.
Miss Nelly Stop interrupting, Bridget. They're just getting to the good bit.
(LUDWIG holds up a ring with a gigantic gemstone set in it)
Heidi A ring! For me? *(takes ring)*
Bridget For her! *(LUDWIG kneels. HEIDI turns away shyly)*
Ludwig I'd like to ask for your ... I mean would you consider ... will you?
Bridget *(raising gun)* Of course I will!
Miss Nelly *(turning to her)* Shut up, Bridget.
Ludwig *(turning to BRIDGET)* I wasn't talking to you. I was ... *(BRIDGET fires the gun. MISS NELLY also comes under the influence)*
Bridget You are in my power!
Ludwig *(hypnotised)* I am in your power ...
Miss Nelly *(turning to LUDWIG)* I am in your power!
Bridget Forget about Heidi ...
Ludwig I've forgotten about Heidi ...
Miss Nelly He's forgotten about Heidi!
Bridget You love only me. *(holds her arms out to him)*
Ludwig I love only you! *(holds his arms out and moves towards BRIDGET)*
Miss Nelly He loves only me!
(MISS NELLY holds her arms out and moves towards LUDWIG. He walks right past her and embraces BRIDGET. MISS NELLY shakes her head and returns to normal)

Ludwig I love you. Je t'adore.

Bridget *(simpering)* Shut it yourself!

Miss Nelly But, your highness ... what about Heidi?

Ludwig Heidi? Who's she? *(Enter PROFESSOR CRACKPOT from the Ballroom)*

Crackpot There you are. Give me back my gun!

Bridget *(giving him the gun)* Take it! I don't need it anymore! *(Exits to the Dungeons)*

Ludwig Where are you going, Brigitte? *(snatching ring from HEIDI)* Give me back my ring! *(following BRIDGET)* Don't leave me, Brigitte! I love you! *(he exits)*

Heidi *(tearfully)* Ludwig!

Miss Nelly *(comforting her)* Men are all the same. Don't worry, he'll be back. He'll realise he's made a terrible mistake. *(Enter LUDWIG and BRIDGET)* You see?

Ludwig I've made a terrible mistake.

Heidi Oh, Ludwig.

Ludwig We shouldn't have gone that way. We should have gone this way. *(they exit quickly upstairs)*

(Enter GIRLS in terror from the Dungeons)

Ethel Run for your lives!

Constance It's Dracula!

Crackpot But what about your peppermints?

Mabel We ate them all! *(The GIRLS dash upstairs)*

Miss Nelly You gutsy little pigs!

Crackpot *(producing bag)* It's alright. I've got some more.

(DRACULA enters from the dungeons, leering and slurping)

Miss Nelly Too late! Run for it! *(MISS NELLY and CRACKPOT follow the GIRLS and all exit in terror)*

Dracula Aren't you going to run away as well?

Heidi No.

Dracula I'll give you a head start.

Heidi Shan't!

Dracula I'm going to bite you!

Heidi Go ahead. *(folds arms and taps foot nonchalantly)*

Dracula Oh, I get it! You're going to whistle for your stupid dog.

Heidi That's right.

Dracula Go ahead. *(folds arms and taps foot nonchalantly)*

Heidi You asked for it. *(to audience)* Come on everybody. Whistle for Kodak. *(ALL whistle. Nothing happens. DRACULA examines his nails)* What's wrong? Why isn't Kodak coming? *(audience responds)* What?

Dracula That's right. You precious pet's been dog-napped! Ha ha!

(Enter GRANULA with KODAK, muzzled and on a lead)

Heidi Kodak!

Granula Your cretaneous canine fell right into our trap.

(DRACULA stalks HEIDI. She backs away to the clock)

Dracula Poor little Heidi! No doggy. No friends. There's nobody to save you now.

Heidi Oh yes there is. *(to audience)* Isn't there?

Audience Yes.

Heidi I'd like to introduce you to a another friend of mine. Dracula ... meet Frankenstein! *(She opens the clock. FRANKIE bashes DRACULA with club and he staggers)*

Dracula Arrgh! Help, granny. It's a monster! *(hides behind GRANULA)*

Granula Leave him alone, you big bully.

Frankie *(displaying false fangs)* What are you going to do about it? Gum me to death?

Granula My choppers! Give them back!

(GRANULA tries to grab them. He clubs her. She staggers behind him. FRANKIE is now positioned between GRANULA and DRACULA)

Granula Waah! *(to DRACULA)* Don't just stand there ... get him!

Dracula Right. *(steps forward)*

Frankie Come on then! *(DRACULA steps back)* You big softy.

Granula My little Dracky can beat you any time he wants to. Can't you?

Dracula No. I mean "yes".

Frankie Prove it, fang-features.

Dracula Anytime, bogey-face.

Frankie I challenge you to a duel. *(slaps his face)* Then we'll see who's the strongest.

Dracula Alright. I accept! *(goes to slap FRANKIE. He ducks and GRANULA gets slapped instead)* A duel it is ... but on one condition ... if I win, Heidi will be mine forever! *(he moves face to face with FRANKIE)*

Frankie It's a deal! *(holds out hand)* Shake on it.

(DRACULA shakes his hand. FRANKIE squeezes. Sound of crunching bones)

Granula Let the duel commence! Dracula versus Frankenstein. Alright, gentlemen, choose your weapons!

Frankie Custard pies at ten paces!

Dracula Fine by me! *(HEIDI hands them two custard pies from the table)*

Granula Stand back to back! *(FRANKIE faces GRANULA and DRACULA faces HEIDI)* When I give the signal, walk ten paces and fire! *(GRANULA moves D.R.)*

Heidi *(to audience)* And you can all be the judges.

Frankie Yes. *(to audience, pointing at DRACULA)* And make sure he doesn't cheat!

Dracula Don't be rotten. *(to audience)* I don't look like a cheater, do I?

Audience Yes.

Granula *(lifting arm)* Ready! Steady! Go! *(drops arm)* One!

(DRACULA turns and follows in step behind FRANKIE as GRANULA slowly counts)

Heidi *(encouraging audience)* Cheat! Cheat!

Granula ... ten!

(FRANKIE stops in front of GRANULA, turns and ducks as DRACULA throws his custard pie. GRANULA gets it in the face and lets go of KODAK. FRANKIE pushes his pie into DRACULA's face)

Frankie I won! I won! *(FRANKIE and KODAK cross to HEIDI)*

Heidi Thank you, Frankie ... you saved my life.

Dracula You cheated!

Heidi *(encouraging audience)* Oh no he didn't.

Granula & Dracula Oh yes he did! *(together)*

Audience Oh no he didn't! *(etc)*

Granula Shut yer traps!

Frankie I won! *(flexing muscles)* I'm much stronger than you!

Dracula Muscles aren't everything. It's much to be better brainy, like me.

Frankie I've got more brains than you!

Dracula Prove it!

Frankie Any time!

Dracula Alright ... I challenge you to another duel!

Frankie Another duel! This time with brains alone! *(ALL exit)*

("Blockbusters" Theme Tune. Change of lighting: main lights dim and effects on, for example 'disco' lights, chasers, mirror-ball. Enter CRACKPOT, BUCKLES, AGNES, MABEL, ETHEL, CONSTANCE and the CHORUS. They quickly reset the stage:

The table is angled to face the audience; the cloth and props are removed to reveal the "Blockbusters" contestants bench underneath; a hand-bell and a hooter are placed on the bench; the three chairs are positioned behind.

A high stool is set centre. ETHEL and CONSTANCE bring on the gameboard D.L. - see Appendix A. BUCKLES positions himself R.C. with two double-sided placards which he will use to prompt the audience: "HOORAY" & "BOO" and "AHHH" & "Whistle". CRACKPOT, AGNES and MABEL carry bags of mints which they will distribute to the audience. The CHORUS sit on the floor to form an onstage audience.

During this, the theme continues and an amplified voice announces the quiz)

Voice Yes it's ... *(current night)* once again at the ... *(local theatre)* here in ... *(town)*. Hello everybody, and welcome to another edition of "Blockbusters". And here is your hostess with the mostest ... Miss Nelly!

(Main lights up. Enter MISS NELLY, flamboyantly attired and carrying a set of question cards. BUCKLES waves the "Hooray" and "Whistle" placards and encourages the audience. AGNES, MABEL and CRACKPOT move among the audience distributing peppermints)

Miss Nelly Thank you. Thank you. *(like an air hostess giving in-flight instructions)* Before we start, we'd like to take the opportunity of offering free peppermint protection to all our patrons. Please note that these lozenges are for emergency use only. In the unlikely event of a Drac-attack, remain seated, wait for the signal ... then suck on your peppermints and blow. Have you got that? How are we doing, Professor?

Crackpot Fine. A few more over here.

Agnes Catch. You dropped it. Butter fingers.

Mabel Some more up here.

Miss Nelly *(to member of audience)* No, no. You're not listening. Don't eat it yet. Save it for an emergency.

Crackpot Some up the back. Get ready. Here they come.

Miss Nelly Careful. You hit that lady right between the eyes.

Agnes A few over here.

Crackpot Everybody who's got a mint, hold it up. Yes, that's enough.

(CRACKPOT, AGNES and MABEL return to the stage. AGNES positions herself behind the contestants bench and takes a prop club. MABEL joins the stage-audience)

Miss Nelly Now remember: we're counting on you so keep your mints in your mitts and not in your mush, till you told. Alright then! It's time to meet our three lucky contestants. Frankenstein ... come on down!

("The Price Is Right" theme music. BUCKLES = "Hooray". FRANKIE appears at the back of the auditorium, shouting excitedly, and dashes for the stage. ALL cheer and applaud hysterically)

Miss Nelly Dracula and Granula ... come on down!

(Music. BUCKLES = "Hooray". DRACULA and GRANULA appear at the back of the auditorium, grinning and waving at the audience. CRACKPOT reverses the sign to "Booo". ALL jeer. DRACULA and GRANULA shake their fists and come to the stage. The contestants take their places behind the bench)

Miss Nelly And last, but by no means least. *(a drumroll)* Let's take a look at tonight's star-prize. Little Orphan Heidi!

(HEIDI enters miserably U.S. and sits meekly on the high-stool. She is trussed up with ribbon and a large bow. BUCKLES = "Whistle". He looks at HEIDI, changes his mind and reverses the sign to "Ahhh". HEIDI hangs her head)

Miss Nelly Ahh. She looks really sad. Let's give her a big "hello" and cheer her up. *(waving at her)* Heidi, hi!

All Ho di ho! *(HEIDI sits up and smiles bravely)*

Miss Nelly O.K. ... before we start, let me remind you of the rules of the contest. *(crosses to the gameboard)* You choose a letter and get a question. Frankenstein, for every correct question, you will get a green space. Join up the greens and you will save our star-prize from a fate worse than death. *(BUCKLES = "Hooray")* But ... if the gruesome twosome manage to connect up the red spaces, poor little orphan Heidi will meet her doom! *(DRACULA and DRACULA jump up and down, cheering. BUCKLES = "Booo")* Yes ... if you get your questions right you can rescue this super, de-luxe orphan ... but if you get your questions wrong, you'll hear this noise *(a two-tone horn)* and you'll get your block busted! *(AGNES whacks each of the contestants over the head: drum-beats. They look pained and rub their heads)* And that's how you play "Blockbusters"! *(a blast of the theme music)* So, without further ado, let's get on with the contest! *(ETHEL points to the letter "S")* We're going to start the with the letter "S". *(she sorts out a question-card)* Hands on your hooters. *(DRACULA and GRANULA hold their noses ... AGNES pulls their hands down and points at the hooter)* Here is your question. *(reading)* What "S" was green and slept for 100 years? *(FRANKIE rings the bell)* Yes, Frankie?

Frankie The Sleeping Bogey!

Miss Nelly Is right! *(BUCKLES = "Hooray". ETHEL removes the "S" hexagon to reveal a green space)* Well done! Vampires, you'll have to be hastier on the hooter. *(to FRANKIE)* Alright, Frankie ... where next?

Frankie "B" please, Nelly.

Miss Nelly A "B". *(consulting card)* Which "B" comes before "hound", "orange", "bank" and "transfusion". *(DRACULA sounds his hooter)* That's Count Drac!

Dracula *(with relish)* Blood!

Miss Nelly Is dead right! *(BUCKLES = "Booo". ETHEL removes "B" from the board revealing a red space)* And here's the first red.

Dracula My favourite colour!

Miss Nelly Where next, Drac? *(DRACULA and GRANULA confer)*

Granula We'll go to "L".

Miss Nelly Good idea. The "L", right at the top there.

Granula This'll be an easy one.

Miss Nelly What "L" is Thomas Tank Engine's favourite dance? *(FRANKIE rings the bell)* Frankie?

Frankie The **Loco**-motion!

Miss Nelly Yes!

SONG L

Ensemble - "The Locomotion"

(ALL jump up and perform a short song and dance routine. The number ends and all return to their original positions as if nothing has happened)

Miss Nelly *(to audience)* Did you like the way we seamlessly slipped that into the plot? *(turning to the board)* Where were we? *(ETHEL reveals a green space)* Oh, yes! Your turn, Frankie. Only one more green and Heidi will be free.

Frankie "R" please, Nelly.

Miss Nelly What "R" is a vampire's favourite breakfast? *(FRANKIE rings the bell)*.

Frankie "Weeta-bites".

Miss Nelly That's not an 'R'!

(BUCKLES = "Ahhh". The horn sounds and AGNES whacks FRANKIE)

Miss Nelly The question goes to the other side. What "R" is a vampire's favourite breakfast? *(GRANULA waves her hand)*

Granula "Ready Neck"!

Miss Nelly You got it!

Granula Yes, we got it ... and we'll get Heidi too! *(BUCKLES = "Booo". A red space is uncovered)*

Miss Nelly Oh dear! Oh dear! Two reds and two greens ... that's neck and neck! *(DRACULA and GRANULA leer)* Where next?

Granula "V".

Miss Nelly What "V" is a vampire's favourite supper?

Dracula *(sounds hooter)* Veins on toast.

Miss Nelly Absolutely right! *(BUCKLES = "Booo". Another red space is uncovered)* Oh dear! This could be where we say goodbye to Heidi ... forever! *(DRACULA and GRANULA rub their hands in glee)* Are you going for it?

Granula We want "M.N."

Miss Nelly I thought you would. This is it, Frankie. *(preening)* Which "M.N." is curvaceous and sexy and fatally attractive to men? *(Smiles and batters her eyelashes. The* *contestants shake their heads and look puzzled. She continues, annoyed)* She's 29 years old and she's standing right in front of you. *(The contestants look around quizzically. She continues, exasperated)* Give them a clue, girls!

(The GIRLS 'sing' a few bars of the "Dallas" theme. DRACULA and GRANULA shake their heads. FRANKIE rings the bell. The GIRLS stop)

Frankie Miss Nelly?

Miss Nelly 100% correct! And that's "Blockbusters"!

(ETHEL removes the "M.N.", connecting up all the green spaces. Theme music and flashing lights. BUCKLES = "Hooray". AGNES clubs DRACULA and GRANULA. They retreat D.S. FRANKIE follows them. ETHEL and CONSTANCE strike the gameboard)

Frankie I'm brainer than you and stronger you.

Dracula You cheated!

Frankie *(to audience)* I won the contest fair and square, didn't I?

Audience Yes.

Granula Mind your own business.

Frankie *(grabbing their ears)* Say you're sorry to the boys and girls.

Dracula Never!

Granula They're rotten little creeps.

Dracula We hate them! *(FRANKIE bashes their heads together and lets go)*

Frankie What do you think I should do with them? *(The audience shout suggestions. FRANKIE moves front and reacts)* What's that? That's a good one ... etc. *(DRACULA and GRANULA start to tip-toe away)*

Miss Nelly Stop them! They're getting away!

Frankie *("Dalek")* Exterminate!

(DRACULA grabs CRACKPOT)

Granula Stay where you are! *(She pulls the hypno-gun from CRACKPOT's pocket and DRACULA tosses him aside. The others gasp)* Keep back.

Frankie Exterminate!

Granula O.K. buster, you asked for it.

(She uses the gun ... bleeps, etc. FRANKIE stops dead in his tracks)

Dracula You're all at our mercy now! *(slurps and drools)*

Heidi Get them, Kodak!

(KODAK attacks. GRANULA fires. He stops in mid-snarl. They move to 'freeze' the others)

Crackpot *(to audience)* Quickly, everybody ... only you can save us now.

Miss Nelly *(to audience)* Yes. It's peppermint time.

Crackpot Stick them in your mouths.

Miss Nelly We'll give them the breath of death!

(DRACULA and GRANULA move D.S. to menace the audience)

Crackpot O.K.?

Both Ready! Steady! Blow!

(ALL blow a 'wind' of peppermint over DRACULA and GRANULA. The gun is dropped. They fall over and roll about gasping)

Dracula Arrgh! Peppermint.

Granula Curses! Curses! *(They stand stagger)*

Miss Nelly One more time.

Crackpot A big deep breath.

Miss Nelly That's it.

Both Blow!

(DRACULA and GRANULA are blown upstage to the Dungeons. There is an explosion and a brief blackout. FRANKIE, KODAK and the others revive. FRANKIE takes the hypno-gun)

Miss Nelly You did it!

Crackpot They've gone forever! *(BUCKLES = "Hooray". HEIDI climbs off the stool)*

Frankie You're safe now, Heidi.

Heidi Yes. Thanks to you. *(indicating audience)* And all our friends. There's only one thing wrong.

Frankie What's that?

Heidi *(struggling to free her arms)* I'm all tied up!

Miss Nelly I forgot about that. We're not finished the show yet. *(to audience)* Now it's time to set Heidi free. And here to cut the ribbon is our very special guest star ... let's have a big hand for Prince Ludwig!

(BUCKLES = "Hooray". Enter PRINCE LUDWIG through Main Door with a champagne bottle, a large pair of scissors and a scroll of paper. HEIDI smiles happily)

Frankie Would you like to do the honours, your highness?

Ludwig *(raising champagne bottle like a club and reading from scroll)* "I name this ship "Heidi", may god bless her and all who sail in ..."

Frankie *(interrupting and taking the champagne bottle)* No, no ... that's the wrong speech!

Ludwig *(turning scroll over)* Oops, sorry. "It gives me great pleasure to declare this maiden 'free'". *(He cuts the ribbons binding HEIDI)*

Heidi *(inclining her cheek to be kissed)* Thank you, Ludwig.

Ludwig *(shaking her hand, platonically)* Don't mention it! *(to ALL)* Attention, everybody. I would like to make an important announcement. *(holding up ring)* I'm getting married to the sweetest, kindest, most generous girl in the whole wide world.

(FRANKIE shakes HEIDI's hand and MISS NELLY shakes LUDWIG's)

Miss Nelly Congratulations!

Ludwig Thank you. I'd like you all to meet *my* future wife and *your* future queen ... Brigitte Bloggs.

(Enter BRIDGET. She is still dressed in her uniform, but also wears a wedding-veil and carries a bouquet)

Bridget *(to BUCKLES)* Let's have three cheers for your queen to be! Hip hip! *(BUCKLES holds up the "Booo" placard. She sniffs huffily)* Huh! *(holding out hand)* Ludwig, the ring!

Ludwig *(flat 'hynotised' voice)* This is for you, my angel. *(puts ring on her finger)*

Bridget Oh, Wiggy ... you shouldn't have! It's so expensive.

Ludwig Nothing is too precious for you, Brigitte.

Bridget *(supporting hand)* Oh ... the diamond's so heavy! *(to HEIDI)* Well, aren't you going to congratulate us?

Heidi Oh ... yes ... congratulations ...

Bridget Thank you. *(loud whisper)* Now buzz off! He's mine now.

Heidi Alright, I'll go. *(she moves D.L. wiping away a tear. BUCKLES = "Ahhh")*

Miss Nelly What are you up to, Bridget?

Bridget "Princess" to you!

Miss Nelly "Princess" my foot!

Bridget You said it! *(stamps on her foot)*

Frankie You can't marry him.

Bridget Why not?

Frankie Because he's in love with Heidi!

Bridget Heidi? Why?

All Ho-di-ho!

Bridget You don't love that ugly little orphan, do you Wiggy?

Ludwig No. I love you. Only you. Forever and ever. My darling.

Frankie You won't get away with this!

Bridget Oh yes I will.

Frankie *(showing hypno-gun)* Oh no you won't! *(He pulls the trigger. LUDWIG stands to attention, mouth agape. To audience)* You can help us. We'll all count to three and snap our fingers. *(to LUDWIG)* And then you'll wake up and follow your heart's desire. One, two, three.

(ALL snap fingers. PRINCE LUDWIG comes out of the trance)

Ludwig What happened? *(he sees HEIDI, who is still moping)* Heidi! *(he rushes to her)* There you are! You're safe! I was so worried about you. *(he takes her hand)*

Heidi Ludwig! You're back to normal at last.

(BRIDGET crosses to them, removing the veil)

Bridget *(giving veil, bouquet and ring to HEIDI)* Here. I won't be needing these any more.

Heidi *(shyly)* He hasn't asked me to marry him.

Ludwig Haven't I? *(kneels)* Heidi, I haven't known you very long, but in that time I have come to realise that you are the only girl that I could possibly ...

All Get on with it!

Ludwig Oh, yes. Will you marry me?

Heidi Of course! *(LUDWIG rises and they embrace)*

Crackpot *(to audience)* Three cheers for the happy couple. Hip Hip.

All Hooray. *(etc)*

(The tabs close leaving FRANKIE and MISS NELLY alone onstage)

End of Scene 1

Act Two
The Songsheet

(FRANKIE and MISS NELLY wave to the others as the tabs close)

Frankie Bye bye.

Miss Nelly See you at the wedding.

Frankie *(to audience)* We'll have a little chat while they're getting ready. Have to enjoyed yourselves? Good. *(to MISS NELLY)* And how about you? Have you had a nice holiday?

Miss Nelly Oh yes. Travelling's so educational ... it widens your frontiers.

Frankie It certainly widened yours!

Miss Nelly Watch it! What about you? Have you ever been abroad?

Frankie No, I've always been a man! I went to Venice once, but I only stayed a few days ... the whole place was flooded! You know, it's the only place in Europe where you can get seasick crossing the street.

Miss Nelly I didn't like Italy ... the men are so rude ... they kept pinching my bottom.

Frankie They'd need a wheelbarrow to pinch that! *(she hits him ... a drum-beat)*

Miss Nelly I prefer France. I had a wonderful time in the City of Love.

Frankie Where's that?

Miss Nelly Paris, of course!

Frankie Oh, Paris. Did you go to the Louvre?

Miss Nelly Oui, oui. I saw Rembrandts and Picassos and Renoirs ...

Frankie All those French cars look the same to me!

Miss Nelly Are you going on holiday next year?

Frankie Yes, I'm going to Greece.

Miss Nelly Ugh, don't bother! I've been there ... it's full of old ruins.

Frankie It must have been if you were there.

Miss Nelly *(huffily)* Oh! I didn't come here to be insulted!

Frankie Where do you usually go? Anyway ... have you had a nice time here?

Miss Nelly Oh yes, Bavaria is really beautiful ... apart from the vampires, of course!

Frankie It's alright now ... we got rid of them, remember?

Miss Nelly *(indicating audience)* Thanks to all our friends. You were fantastic!

Frankie No they weren't. *(produces the false fangs)* They were **fang**-tastic! *(sings and clacks the dentures)* "I'm a little vampire in the night,
Eyes of red and fangs of white ..."

Miss Nelly What's that you're singing?

Frankie It's a song I made up. Shall I teach it to you?

Miss Nelly Why not?

Frankie *(to audience)* Would you all like to learn it too?

Audience Yes.

Frankie That's good. Just by sheer coincidence, I've got all the words written out. *(Enter two of the GIRLS with the Songsheet)* Here they are. Can you read that? Good. I'll sing it first, then you can copy me.

SONG M

"I'm A Little Vampire"

(tune of "I'm A Little Teapot")

I'm a little vampire in the night
(flap arms) Eyes of red and fangs of white!
(point at eyes) (use forefingers as fangs)
When the sun is shining, you're alright
(palms up, look skyward) (thumbs up)
But when it's dark I bite, bite, bite!
(cover eyes) ('bite' with hands)

(The song is learnt by the audience and performed a few times. Volunteer children are invited onstage to help with the song and are interviewed. The audience is divided in two and a 'competition' is held to see who can sing the loudest)

Miss Nelly That was good fun ... but I've got to dash and get ready for the Royal Wedding! Bye bye!

(FRANKIE distributes sweets to the 'volunteers' who return to their seats. There is one final chorus of the Songsheet and ALL exit as the tabs open for the Finale)

Act Two
Finale

(The stage is clear of props and furniture and the CHORUS and DANCERS are onstage for the walkdown number)

SONG N
The Walkdown

(The CHORUS and DANCERS come forward in small groups, bow and move back leaving centre-stage clear. ALL carry flags. The principals enter:
(1) KODAK and BUCKLES. They bow and then BUCKLES gives KODAK a bone.
2) HERR & FRAU PUMPERNICKEL. She is wearing a new hat and he carries a money-bag with a large "£" sign on it. They bow. She pats her hat and he clasps the money bag to his heart.
3) AGNES, MABEL, ETHEL and CONSTANCE (with book). They cheer as they run D.S. ETHEL and CONSTANCE bow ... AGNES and MABEL kick their bottoms and are chased to the side.
4) PROFESSOR CRACKPOT and BRIDGET, arm in arm. They bow. PROFESSOR CRACKPOT puts a ring on BRIDGET's finger and she simpers.
5) DRACULA and GRANULA, shaking their fists. They bow deeply. GRANULA can't straighten up again and has to be helped to the side.
6) FRANKIE (with fangs). He enters stiffly, arms outstretched and stomps part of the way D.S. before breaking into a run and bowing.
7) MISS NELLY in an outrageous costume. She bows and blows kisses to the audience.
8) PRINCE LUDWIG and HEIDI, in wedding attire. ALL cheer and wave their flags.
(The song ends and the principals move forward for the final couplets. The line up, from stage left to right, should be: KODAK, HERR PUMPERNICKEL, AGNES, ETHEL, PROFESSOR CRACKPOT, BRIDGET, FRANKIE, HEIDI, PRINCE LUDWIG, MISS NELLY, DRACULA, GRANULA, MABEL, CONSTANCE, FRAU PUMPERNICKEL and BUCKLES.
BUCKLES holds up his hands to silence the audience)

Buckles We hope that you enjoyed the show.
Crackpot We hope you found it funny.
Frau Pump And if you didn't, that's too bad!
Herr Pump 'Coz I've got all your money! *(shakes money-bag)*
Dracula I lost the games of brain and brawn
I didn't get the prize! *(points at HEIDI)*
Miss Nelly Well here's a consolation gift ...
Dracula What's that?
Miss Nelly A bunch of fives! *(shakes fist at DRACULA)*
Granula But I can still chew Heidi up:
I'll chomp and bite and bash her.
Frankie You'll have to use your gums, I fear
'Coz I've still got your gnashers! *(shows fangs)*
Heidi Poor Bridget never caught her prince.
Ludwig Oh what a shame, god bless her!
Bridget Don't you worry, I'm alright:
I've married the Professor! *(she pats his head)*

Agnes So, "Auf wiedersehen", as they say in France.
Ethel Which means "you've had your lot"!
Constance That's not what it says in this here book!
Mabel Oh, shut up you, little swot!

SONG O

(Supplementary Lyrics)

We're glad that you came
'Coz you were so trusting:
You gave us a hand
When blocks needed busting!
When things look black
Your help will always see us through:
We don't need anything but you!

Granula was disgusting!
Dracula was a rat!
But you stopped their blood-lusting:
One mint and that was that!

Our story is done:
We're taking our bow now.
We hope you had fun:
It's time to go home now.
Remember one last thing before we say "adieu":
We don't need anything but you!

The End

Appendix A - Production Notes

This production uses one basic, "semi" box-set which can be adapted for each of the full-stage scenes. The doors and windows are interchangeable and the overall appearance is modified by lighting and 'dressing'. Only half the stage is 'boxed', leaving the D.S. area free for entrances, furniture and scenic tabs. There are no scene changes in Act II and it is therefore possible to either use double-sided flats and reverse them, or reposition the set during the interval to completely change the appearance.

The stage plans below are for guidance only. The set can be made more complex, for example, by adding rostra to create different acting levels, using revolves ... or it could be further simplified by using arches instead of practical doors and dispensing with the stairs. Scenic backcloths, though less effective, could be used as an alternative.

Act I - Scene 1

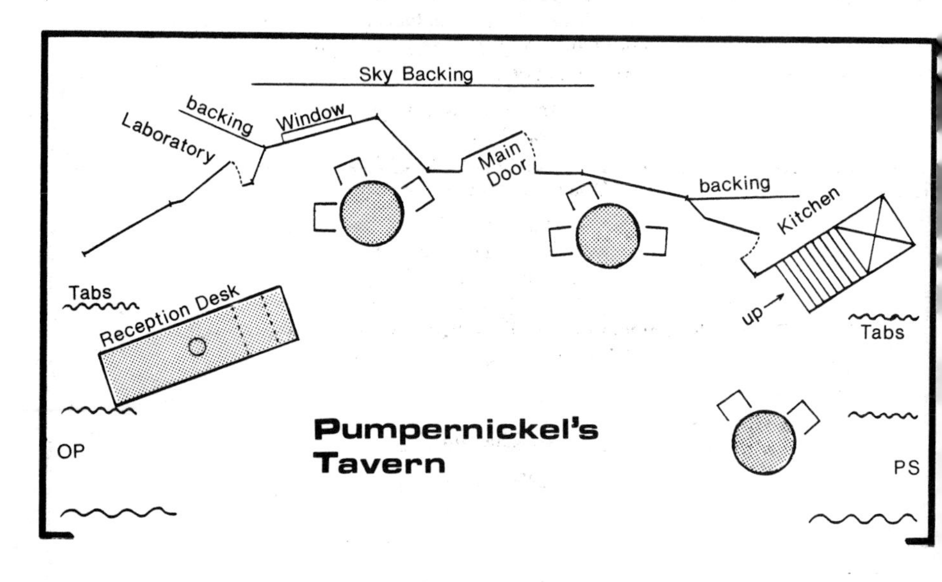

The Tavern Sign: Painted on hardboard in three sections: : 1. *PUMPER* 2. *NICKEL* 3. *'S* and hung over the door on hooks.

The Reception Desk & Bar can also function used as the Dining Table and Contestant's Bench in Act II. It must have room for access underneath. Two false-fronts are required: 1) with a wooden panel design (bar) and 2) with a pattern of large hexagons - red at Dracula's side and green at the other. A hole, big enough for a head, should be cut in the top surface and covered when not in use. The tablecloth should also have "head" hole and the Dining Table should be fully draped.

Frankie's Bucket: Cut at least 1.5 metre lengths of fine material, plastic or paper and glue at the bottom of the bucket. Metallic finishes will look, momentarily, like water and will therefore create a better effect. Use confetti as an alternative.

The Hypno-gun: Could be any weirdly-decorated toy gun ... for example, brightly painted, decorated with glitter and sequins, with feathers or a child's windmill in the barrel, etc. "Space-guns" are available in toy shops which have built in "beeping" sound effects and flashing lights.

Act I - Scene 2

Granula's False Fangs: A real pair of false teeth would be ideal but may be hard to come by! "Novelty Shops" often stock joke teeth, or they could be made with wire and papier maché. Granula only pretends to insert them. Use castinets to create a 'clacking' sound effect.

Act 1 - Scene 3

There are three alternative ways of staging this scene:
1) Use a scenic back-cloth and a single window flat positioned at one side of the stage.
2) If no traverse tabs are available for the scenic cloth, light only the front half of the stage and use a book flat or screen, with window, to partially mask the box-set.
3) Use the same full-set as Scene 1, repositioning and/or masking the doors and windows. Strike the stairs.

The Bats: can be a simple construction of black paper. Attach to wires so that they can be "invisibly" operated from below or the side.

Act 1 - Scene 5

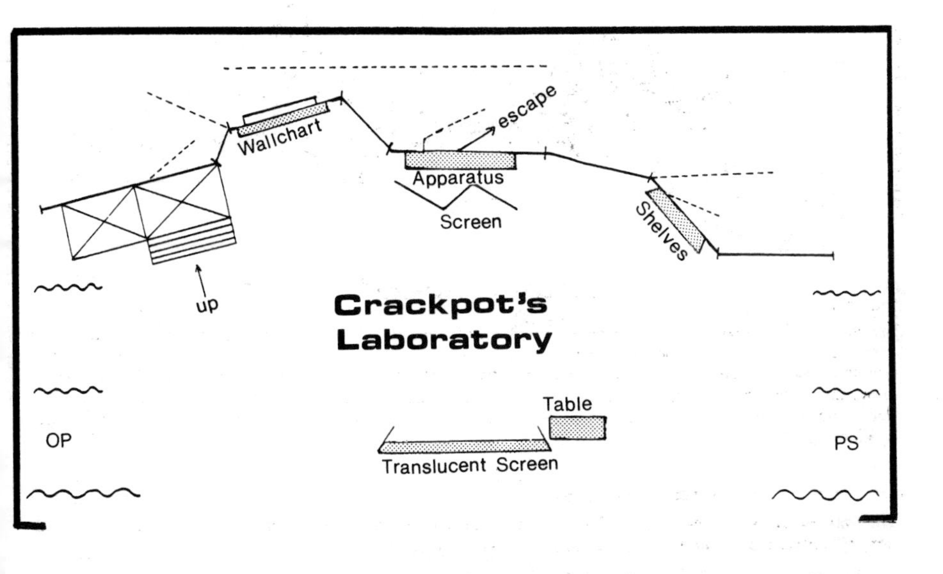

The Translucent Screen can be made from white sheeting stretched over a frame.

The Head and Hand: Latex heads and hands can be purchased from a 'joke' shop. Alternatively, make the props with papier maché:
1) Steep shredded newspaper in boiling water. Add detergent to remove excess printer's ink and leave over-night. 2) Strain through a colander and rinse. 3) Allow to drain. Gently press out any excess water. 4) Mash the paper to a 'doughy' consistency. 5) Add a small amount of cellulose, wallpaper adhesive straight from the packet. Use rubber gloves and mix to a pulp. 6) Model the head on a polystyrene wig/hat base which has been coated with vaseline. Allow to dry thoroughly. 7) Cut the head in two and remove it carefully from the base. Use strips of glued paper to join the two halves. 8) A fine surface can be obtained by sand-papering or by pasting on

strips of tissue paper. 9) Use an undercoat of white emulsion to seal the surface before painting the features. A final coat of matt varnish will strengthen the finished head.

The hand can be constructed from wire (plastic-coated garden wire is ideal) and then covered with strips of pasted-paper until the desired shape is achieved. Allow to dry. Paint and varnish as above.

The Prop Mallet: The head of the mallet can be made from a shaped block of foam. Cut a slit through the centre and wedge it onto a glued, wooden handle. Caution: Use a non-solvent adhesive ... some plastic foams react to solvents.

The Bolts through Frankie's neck can be made from two toilet roll tubes, painted silver. Mount the tubes on a girl's plastic hair-band. This will clip easily round the neck and will be invisible if painted to match Frankie's make-up.

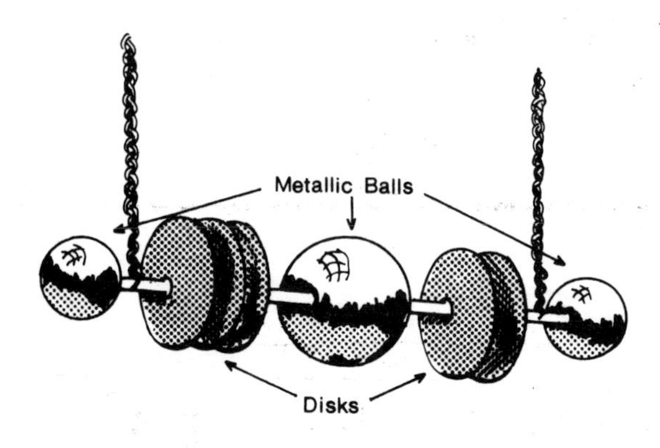

The Transformation Apparatus: The illustration above is based on part of the apparatus used in the original film version of "Frankenstein" and represents a lightning conductor. It can be constructed from a wooden pole, cardboard discs and balls. The whole contraption should be painted silver and highlighted with glitter ... use a non-solvent impact adhesive for glitter (solvents dissolve the shine). The "conductor" should be suspended above the trolley and the rest of the apparatus can be a jumble of wires, tubes, dials, wheels, chains ... anything that comes to hand. "Chaser lights" would be particularly effective and can be hired from any theatrical/disco lighting supplier.

Act II - Scene 1

The Stained-Glass Window: Make a frame to fit the main door. Pieces of coloured gel joined with black vinyl tape will give the impression of a leaded, stained-glass window.

The Throne: must be large enough to allow access from the back of the set through the hinged seat. A simple box with a hinged lid could be used as an alternative.

The Clock: Construct from plywood on a wooden, coffin-shaped frame. Alternatively, make an oblong frame and an overlapping, coffin-shaped front. The clock-face should be hinged so that it can open independently. Cut a 'hand' hole in the front. The back section should be hinged at the bottom (opening outwards) for access or masked with black velvet. *(See diagram below)*

The Dining Table & Contestant's Bench: *see "Reception Desk" above.*

Heidi's Ribbon can be joined with at the back velcro. She can free herself by raising her arms when Ludwig 'cuts' the ribbon.

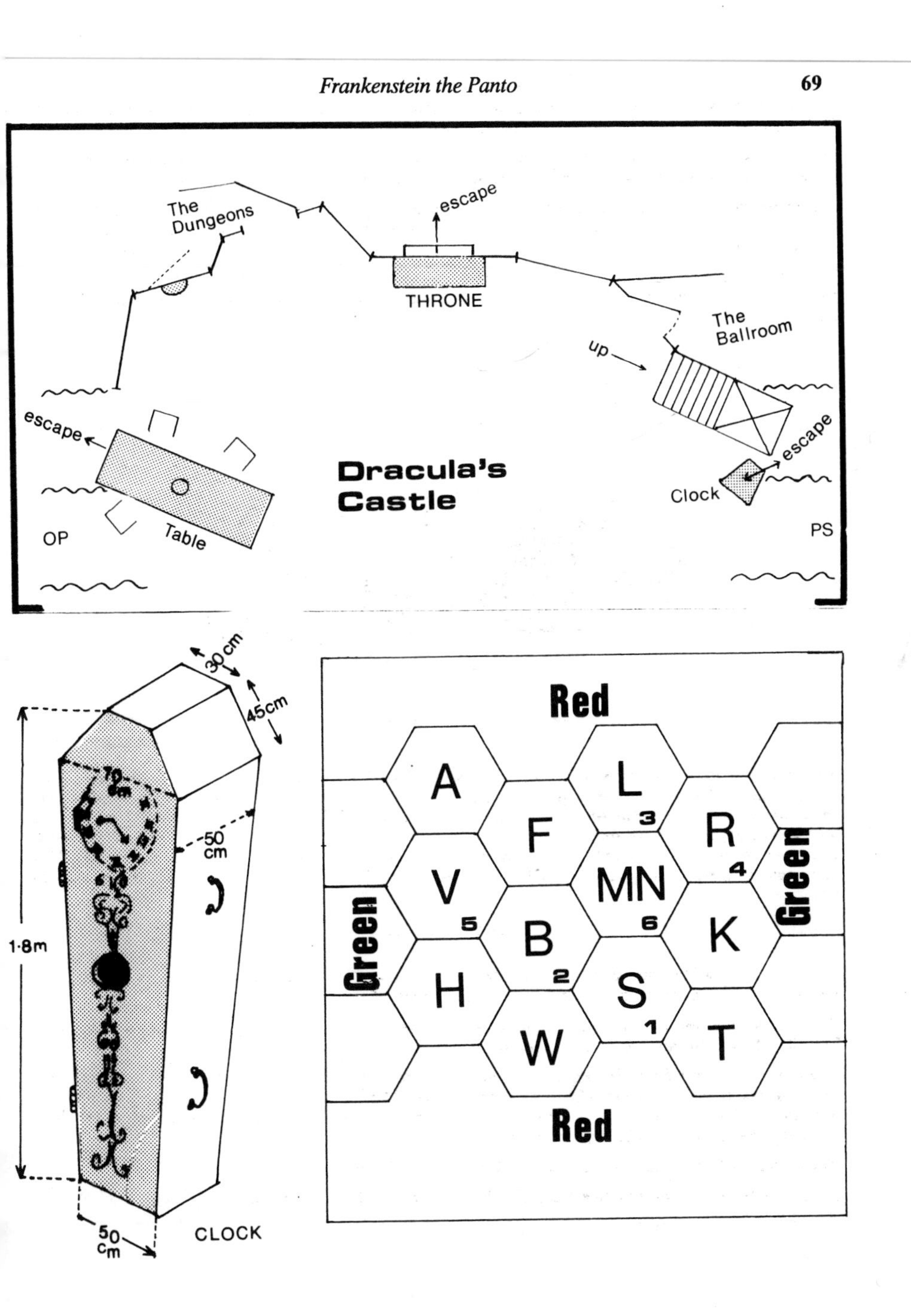
The Dungeons
escape
THRONE
The Ballroom
up
escape
escape
Dracula's Castle
Clock
OP
Table
PS
30cm
45cm
1·8m
50 cm
50 cm
CLOCK
Red
A
L
3
F
R
V
4
MN
Green
Green
5
6
B
K
H
2
S
1
W
T
Red

The Game Board: The object of the game is to connect a line of red or green hexagons by answering questions correctly ... see Miss Nelly's explanation in the script.

Use a sheet of hardboard and mark it out as shown. Paint the shaded area green and red (see diagram) these are the winning hexagon's. The remainder of the hexagons should be painted white.

Cut out white, cardboard hexagons to mask the red and green ones. These can be attached to the board with velcro. Letter **all** the white hexagons as shown (the numbers indicate the order of the correct answers). As the game progresses, Ethel removes the appropriate white hexagon to reveal the winning colour beneath.

A more elaborate (and expensive) board could be made from a sheet of plastic (available in D.I.Y. stores). Use white emulsion, white card and red & green gels. When lit from behind, the red and green hexagons will "light-up" as the white ones are removed.

Appendix B - Lighting Plot

Act One - Scene 1

No.	Cue	Page
To open	*Bright interior, sunny exterior*	1
1	**Ludwig:** ... And goodness will vanish with the sun! *Exterior lights - creep to sunset*	8
2	**Heidi:** We forgot the front door. *Lightning - exterior blackout.*	19
3	The tabs close *Fade out.*	20

Act One - Scene 2

No.	Cue	Page
To open	*Exterior, night & follow spots*	20

Act One - Scene 3

No.	Cue	Page
To open	*Candlelit interior*	
4	(MISS NELLY blows the candle out) *gloomy interior*	27

Act 1 - Scene 4

No.	Cue	Page
To open	*gloomy interior*	28

Act 1 - Scene 5

No.	Cue	Page
To open	*Gloomy interior*	32
5	**Crackpot:** Lights! *Dim main lights, floodlight behind translucent screen*	32
6	**Crackpot:** Lights! *Floodlight off, return main lights*	32
7	**Miss Nelly:** "Electricity" to you. *Lights flicker*	35
8	**Heidi:** ... something terrible's about to happen at any minute. *Lights flicker*	35
9	**Heidi:** Yes, it's a bit of mess. *Lights flicker*	35
10	**Granula:** Now where are they? *Lights flicker*	36

11	**Crackpot:** I've just learnt to snap my fingers! *Lights flicker*	37
12	**Crackpot:** Hey Presto! *Lights flicker*	38
13	(CRACKPOT pulls the lever) *Flashing lights*	38

Act Two - Scene 1

To open	*Very dim interior* *Sunlight through stained-glass window*	41
14	(During opening number) *Creep lights up*	41
15	**Frankie:** Come on, everybody. *Lights up - gloomy interior*	41
16	(AGNES touches the newspaper) *Fade light through stained-glass window.* *Follow spot to clock face and throne.*	44
17	(GRANULA steps out of the throne) *Follow spot off*	45
18	(Chase around auditorium & return to stage) *House lights on and off.*	49
19	**Frankie:** This time with brains alone. *Dim main-lights. Special effects*	57
20	(Enter MISS NELLY) *Main-lights up. Effects off. House lights on.*	58
21	(CRACKPOT, AGNES & MABEL return to stage) *House lights off*	58
22	**Miss Nelly:** Frankenstein, come on down! *Effects on and off*	58
23	**Miss Nelly:** Dracula and Granula, come on down! *Effects on and off*	58
24	**Miss Nelly:** And that's how you play "Blockbusters"! *Effects on and off*	59
25	**Miss Nelly:** 100% correct. And that's "Blockbusters"! *Effects on and off.*	60
26	(DRACULA and GRANULA are blown U.S.) *Brief blackout*	61

Act Two - Songsheet

To open	*Front lights*	63

Act Two - Finale

To open	*Full lights and effects.*	65

Appendix C - Effects Plot

Act One - Scene 1

No.	Cue	Page
1	(FRANKIE clouts Herr Pumpernickel) *Drum beat*	2
2	**Herr Pump:** Orphans? *Soulful music*	2
3	(FRANKIE throws the contents of the bucket ...) *Cymbal*	5
4	**All:** Dracula! *Sinister fanfare*	8
5	(PROFESSOR CRACKPOT uses the hypno-gun) *Electronic beeping*	9
6	**Others:** What's that? *Bubbling noises*	12
7	**Miss Nelly:** Heel, girls! *A ripping noise*	15
8	(Enter PRINCE LUDWIG) *A fanfare*	17
9	**Girls:** Dracula! *Sinister fanfare*	18
10	**Ludwig:** Peppermints haven't been invented yet! *Explosion and smoke*	18
11	**Heidi:** We forgot to lock the front door. *Loud thunder*	19

Act One - Scene 3

No.	Cue	Page
12	**Agnes:** You're driving us bats! *Squeaking*	23
13	(BRIDGET drops shoe out of window) *Swannee whistle*	23
14	MISS NELLY does strip routine *Music - "The Stripper"*	25
15	AGNES thrusts leg out and pulls it back *Swannee whistle each time*	25
16	(The trunk opens and clothes thrown out) *Swannee whistle each time*	26
17	**Miss Nelly:** Phooey! *Squeaking*	27
18	(MISS NELLY blows the candle out) *Eerie music & squeaking followed by thunder and a flash*	27
19	**Granula:** I've found an open window. *Squeaking*	27
20	DRACULA holds hands out, mesmerising *Soft, eerie music*	28

Act One - Scene 4

No.	Cue	Page
21	**Granula:** And let my dentures chomp and bite! *Drum-roll*	30
22	(... the teeth bite FRANKIE's bottom) *Cymbals*	30
23	**Frankie:** Has anyone got an Elastoplast? *Ambulance siren*	30
24	**Crackpot:** Quickly. To the laboratory! *Ambulance siren*	31

Act One - Scene 5

25	(MISS NELLY whacks patient over the head) *Drum-thud*	33
26	(Patient raises legs/torso) *"Boing" sound effects*	33
27	(CRACKPOT makes incision with knife) *"Zipper" sound effect*	33
28	(CRACKPOT drills the head) *"Dentist's drill" sound effect*	33
29	(CRACKPOT drills the stomach) *"Pneumatic drill" sound effect*	33
30	(MISS NELLY falls over) *Drum-thud*	33
31	(CRACKPOT continues delving) *"Plopping" noises*	33
32	(MISS NELLY plays reveille) *Bugle*	33
33	(The bugle is tossed over the screen) *Telephone ringing*	33
34	(MISS NELLY thumps patient on head) *Drum-thud*	34
35	(PROFESSOR CRACKPOT saws the head off) *"Sawing - wood" sound effect*	34
36	(He drops the saw and unscrews the head) *"Squeaking" followed by "Pop"*	34
37	(He bolts on the head) *Metallic squeaks*	34
38	(... the patient's finger rests on the record ...) *Max Bygraves' music*	34
39	**Miss Nelly:** Seeing how near the storm is. *Thunder*	35
40	**Heidi:** ... four, five. *Thunder*	35
41	**Heidi:** ... three, four. *Thunder*	35
42	**Heidi:** ... two, three. *Thunder*	36
43	(AGNES steps behind GRANULA) *Ripping noise*	37
44	**Crackpot:** One. Two. *Thunder*	37
45	(CRACKPOT pulls the lever) *Puff of smoke*	38

Act Two - Scene 1

To open	*Smoke & spooky effects*	41
46	**Miss Nelly:** Enchanté, m'sieur! *Waltz music*	42
47	**Agnes:** Someone pinch her, please. *Drumroll*	43
48	(the hand pinches BRIDGET) *Cymbal*	43
49	(ETHEL leans forward and is pinched ! *Drumroll and cymbal*	43
50	**Mabel:** You'd better not ... there wouldn't be much left ! *Electric vehicle and bottles rattling*	43

51	**Constance:** There was a spook, wasn't there? *Bicycle bell*	43
52	(AGNES touches the newspaper) *Clock chimes*	44
53	**Agnes:** Send for reinforcementes ! *Alarm clock ringing*	45
54	(GRANULA hits the alarm clock) *springs breaking*	45
55	(LUDWIG lifts the food cover) *Maniacal laughter*	47
56	(FRANKIE drops clock into throne) *Swannee whistle & distant crash*	47
57	**Dracula:** ... in the whole wide world can defeat us now! *Waltz music*	48
58	**Buckles:** Why not? *Waltz music*	48
59	**Bridget:** Walls have ears! *Approaching footsteps*	49
60	**All:** ... BINGO! *Flash & loud explosion*	50
61	(PROFESSOR CRACKPOT uses the hypno-gun) *Electronic beeping*	51
62	(FRANKIE hits GRANULA) *Swannee whistle and crash*	52
63	(BRIDGET uses the hypno-gun) *Electronic beeping*	53
64	**Frankie:** Shake on it. *Sound of cracking bones*	55
65	**Frankie:** ... this time with brains alone! *"Blockbusters" theme*	57
66	**Miss Nelly:** Frankenstein, come on down! *"The Price is Right" theme*	58
67	**Miss Nelly:** Dracula and Granula, come on down! *"The Price is Right" theme*	58
68	**Miss Nelly:** Little Orphan Heidi! *Drum-roll*	59
69	**Miss Nelly:** If you get your questions wrong ... this noise! *Two-tone horn*	59
70	**Miss Nelly:** And that's how you play "Blockbusters"! *"Blockbusters" theme*	59
71	**Miss Nelly** That's not an 'R'! *Two-tone horn*	60
72	**Miss Nelly** 100% correct. And that's "Blockbusters"! *"Blockbusters" theme and horn.*	60
73	(GRANULA uses the hypno gun) *Electronic noises*	61
74	(DRACULA and GRANULA are blown U.S.) *Flash*	61
75	(FRANKIE uses the hypno gun) *Electronic noises*	61

Appendix D - Furniture and Properties List

Act One - Scene 1

On stage Main Door with *Pumpernickel's Taverna* Sign, Door with *Kitchen* sign, Door with *Lab* sign
Window (**Tavern**), Stairs
Signs: *Credit..., No nose blowing..., Rooms..., Cash Only..., Menu...*
Mirror, Tables (with cloths and plates) & Chairs
2 buckets (*one with streamers*) and mops
Bar/Reception Desk, *on it:* "Happy Hour" sign, a hand bell, beer steins
under it: "Reception" sign, a calculator, a ledger

Personal Tray with beer steins **(Heidi)**
Trays of food (**Frau Pumpernickel & Frankie**)
Bank notes, handkerchief (**Herr Pumpernickel**)
Walking stick (**Buckles**)
Monocle, scroll (**Prince Ludwig**)
Spectacles, black light-bulb, teabag, hypno-gun (**Crackpot**)
Phrasebook, bag, passport (**Miss Nelly**)
Bags & violin cases, hockey sticks (**Schoolgirls**)
Make-up bag (**Bridget**)
Book (**Constance**)
Bubblegum (**Mabel**)
Spectacles (**Constance**)
Miss Nelly's bloomers, Frankie's & Dracula's underpants (**Agnes**)

Off stage Towel (*in kitchen*)
Two hats, handbag containing photograph and pen (**Frau Pumpernickel**)

Act One - Scene 2

Personal Walking stick, false-fangs (**Granula**)

Act One - Scene 3

On stage Bed (**with sheet**) and three pillows
Trunk
Candle

Personal Book (**Constance**)
Mirror & perfume (**Bridget**)

Off stage Bats (**Stage Management**)

Act One - Scene 4

Off stage Hospital trolley (**Crackpot**)
on it: Giant syringe, "ZZZ" sign, sheet

Act One - Scene 5

On stage Stairs (*masking Lab Door*), Wall chart (*masking window*),
Transformation apparatus (*masking Main Door*), Decorated Screen
Racks of bottles, books etc. (*masking Kitchen Door)*
Translucent screen, *behind it:* 2 pairs boxing gloves, tube of material, garden shears, bunch of flowers, wellington boot, prop hand, bugle, telephone receiver, birthday cake, prop head, a mirror
A table, *On it:* Carving knife & steel, mallet, socks, drill, saw, washing-up bowl, "Fairy Liquid", spanner & bolts, L.P. record

Off stage Surgical mask (**Crackpot**)
Mops, wigs & overalls (**Granula & Dracula**)
Hockey sticks (**Schoolgirls**)
Green bloomers (**Agnes**)

Act Two - Scene 1

On stage

Wall section with hole (*over Lab Door*)
Arch & "Dungeons" sign (*original window*)
Stained glass window (*original Main Door*)
Sign "The Ballroom (*Kitchen Door*)
Dining table with hole
On it: crockery, glass, candelabra, silver food cover, 2 custard pies, club, flowers, condiments
Granfather clock
Throne, Alarm clock
Ladies slippers (**Granula**)

Personal

Prop club (**Frankie**)
Book (**Constance**)
Milkbottles (**Milkman**)
Bicycle, bag & newspaper (**Newsboy**)
Mallet (**Granula**))
Dressing gown & bed cap (**Dracula**)
Tattered lab coat, hypno-gun, bag of peppermints (**Crackpot**)
Diamond ring (**Ludwig**)
False fangs (**Frankie**))

Off stage

Skeleton & politician mask (**Stage management**)
Butterfly net (**Granula**) Fishing rod with bone (**Dracula**) Sticks of dynamite (**Agnes**)
Detonator box with plunger (**Mabel**)
Coil of wire (**Ethel**)
Cup & saucer (**Stage management**)
Tattered costume (**Miss Nelly**)
Cleaning items (**Schoolgirls**)
Dog lead & muzzle (**Granula**)
A hand bell, a hooter (**Stage managment**)
High stool (**Heidi**)
Bags of mints (**Crackpot, Mabel, Agnes**) Game-board (**Constance & Ethel**)
Placards (**Buckles**)
Question cards (**Miss Nelly**)
Ribbon & bow (**Heidi**)
Champagne bottle, scroll, scissors (**Prince Ludwig**)
Wedding veil, bouquet, hypno-gun (**Bridget**)

Act Two - Songsheet

Off stage

Songsheet (**Stage management**)
Sweets (Frankie)

Act Two - Finale

Personal

Bone (**Buckles**)
New hat (**Frau Pumpernickel**)
Money bag (**Herr Pumpernickel**)
Book (**Constance**)
Ring (**Professor Crackpot**)
False fangs (**Frankie**)
Flags (**Chorus & Principals**)